DIVERSE VOICES

DIVERSE VOICES:

ESSAYS ON POETS AND POETRY

BY MARK RUDMAN

STORY LINE PRESS
1993

ISBNs: 0-934257-67-1 cloth, 0-934257- 68-X paper

Published by Story Line Press, Inc., Three Oaks Farm, Brownsville, OR 97327

This publication was made possible thanks in part to the generous support of the Nicholas Roerich Museum, the Andrew W. Mellon Foundation, the National Endowment for the Arts and our individual contributors.

ACKNOWLEDGEMENTS
Grateful acknowledgment is made to the editors of the following magazines, in which the essays first appeared:

The American Poetry Review, "Mexican Mosaic," "Homer in Our Time" (from "On Translation"); *Boulevard*, "Mosaic on Walking"; *Denver Quarterly*, "On 'On Location'," "Letters: Summer 1926, Angelic Orders, Spare Moments," "James Schuyler's Changing Skies"; *Ironwood*, "Open and Closed Space," "No Longer in Continuous Time," "Sometimes a Painful Existing"; *The Nation*, "A Calm and Clear Eye," "'Car, Bomb, God'," "Dour Panache," "Snapshots of the Soul,"; *The New York Times Book Review*, "Questions About Questions"; *Pequod*, "A Response to Heidegger's *Poetry, Language, and Truth*"; *Poetry East*, "Word Roots: On Free Verse"; *Threepenny Review*, "Some Thoughts on Letters and Poetry," "On Notebooks," "On Translation: Dostoyevsky in English"

And the following anthologies: *Best American Essays 1991*, ed. Joyce Carol Oates and Robert Atwan, "Mosaic on Walking"; *Conversant Essays*, ed. James McCorkle, "Word Roots: On Free Verse"

Thanks are due Celia Bland, Jean Gordon, and Deirdre Day MacCloud for help in preparation of the manuscript.

I would also like to thank Elaine Epstein, Rachel Hadas, Jan Heller Levi, and Katherine Washburn for their scrutiny of various versions of these pages. Special thanks to Michael Cuddihy and Adam Gopnik. And I am indebted to Chris Benfey and Ruth Mathewson without whose help some of these essays would not have found their final form.

for Madelaine

CONTENTS

Balmy Saturday afternoon. Early March. Walking the promenade in Riverside Park I see a lanky woman, blond, running a baby carriage around in a circle, away from a skinny curly-headed bearded man. "Won't someone help me," she pleads. "This is my baby and he's trying to take him away from me. Won't someone help me." The man holds the carriage still; and, moving with deliberate slowness, kneels down in front of the baby and reaches for his chin. The woman shouts, backpedaling, tugging the carriage. . . . A group converges, circling the carriage. The man stands up and faces them. "You're not the police, what are you gonna do?" I believe the woman's story but the man isn't harming her or the baby at this moment. "He beats me up and now he wants to take the baby away from me." Two women escort the woman off. The man keeps vaulting between them to walk alongside the carriage. Brutal, the form of his persistence. And as if a series of screens had been transposed momentarily over the scene I think of my father's stories of my mother's attempts to prevent him from seeing me in weekend street encounters like this, and my mother's accounts of his stubbornness. My loyalties are divided—by a hair's breadth. Paralyzed, I watch them move away from the river and keep them in sight just in case, until they disappear.

No accident that I find so resonant this line of Henri Michaux: *I will intervene.*

*

In this season I am often sulky, sullen, restless, withdrawn. I feel transparent, as if inhabited by the weather.

Only while walking am I relieved from distress, only then, released from the burden of self, am I free to think. I wanted to say walking brings relief from tension without sadness and then I think it is not so—these walks bring their own form of *tristesse.* There is discomfort when movement stops.

Though not exceptionally tall (a shade under six feet) I am a rangy, rambly walker. I take up a lot of space!

I know when I emphasize strolling and walking that I am pointing to a crisis in leisure time, my own, everyone's. We know what Wordsworth and Whitman and James did with their afternoons: they walked, with and without direction, destination.

Raw wind bites my neck. I have lost three scarves in the past ten days and feel the cold season won't last long enough for me to buy another.

*

The sponge, not the shell, is our model. The armor that protects us is prelude to our downfall.

I choose this surly, inbetween season, precisely because its inhospitability to walking provides a frame, limits possibility. I won't be tempted to overload. And a burden

of work to be done makes me fantasize a more lei-
surely, unstressed pace.

*

This Sunday evening, walking by the street where my
friend X no longer lives, it seems strangely flattened
out, straight, sober, for all its literal ups and downs,
and in spite of the unbroken downslope toward the
Hudson. No longer a text, no longer tortured. Maybe
the street took on the attributes of X's search, his complicated, conflicted grasp and apprehension, his sense
that the world (as text) was riddled with meanings.
And now that he has gone it has become—just a street!
The streetlamps have withdrawn from their contortions.
These once expressionist streets have become stage-
sets for the weekly T.V. series, *The Equalizer*. (X never
owned, will never own a television.) Crowds cluster
around red chalk body outlines. Megaphones threaten.

These are the dangers of walking in a familiar city.
Our unconscious dogs us like a double. Associations
will rise unbidden from their coffers and containers. I
can't seem to walk anywhere of late without this happening to me. Each neighborhood conceals a reposi-
tory of framed images, old lovers, old friends, framed
that is until they begin to unravel. When I walk by the
apartments in the Village where I used to live and glance
through the black rusted railings into the underground
window, I imagine that I will be there, in that room, as I
was ten years ago, raving and pacing.

A look in the real window below brings me back to
reality. The bedroom's been converted into an office. I
fantasize a lot about travel but I may time travel here

more than I would in any unfamiliar place because when I am transported back to that place and time I am also seeing it through a prism: who I was then through who I am now, then that double perspective on whoever I am remembering, then their perspective. That's a figure with at least six sides.

There is an unresolved mystery about those relationships with old lovers that still fascinates me though, once I am back there. Mutual cruelties. Or how much of it broke down into this binary split: I love her more than she loves me; she loves me more than I love her.

*

Walking in Manhattan, I feel as if my past were riding alongside me on an outrigger.

*

My horror of leaving New York is bound up with the loss of walking space.

The blocks grow longer as you move west. The streets are too wide. The places we lived in the Southwest when I was a boy, Salt Lake City, Colorado Springs, were always surrounded, hemmed in, by mountains. Suddenly, looking up and around I'd feel dwarfed by the immensity of the sky, and squeezed by the sense of bound distances, enclosures. I began to see everything in terms of its distance from the sea. The only other people on the block were so far away they could have been in another county.

In Manhattan I am aware at every moment that the tall buildings are man-made structures. Even the shoddy scaffolding of a new hotel going up can be reassuring.

We know we're being measured by our life's terms, finite pressures, mortality, not the blank eternal gaze of sea and sky and mountain.

*

When my mother and I lived in Las Vegas, during the time she was getting her divorce, the desert was still across the street, opposite the strip. After dinner I'd drag her toward my favorite destination—a gulley about a quarter-mile into the desert. It came after rows of cacti. I would submit to bed only after I returned in the dusk to test their prickliness; I would try to move my fingers around the spines and press through the pulp to the sticky water without drawing blood. She'd never say we had to go back because it was getting dark, only because it was getting cold—which it was. I loved these succulents, which managed to survive on what seemed to be so little water (though the measurement was only by our standards).

*

Walking to a midtown lunch I go by the building where my grandfather lived, and my mother and I lived for a time when I was a child. Heading downtown, the same afternoon, I pass the building where my father worked. I feel both haunted and vacant. Within ten minutes, moving from the East Side, just shy of the park, to the West, I can walk past Hortense Court, the building my great-grandmother designed and the building on the other side of town where my father lived. Myriad associations follow. Only once, twice a year does it occur to me that I live within blocks of where I lived when I was an infant. Being driven inward even while I walk exhausts me. I find consolation in Pavese's idea that there's no one who has not sprung from the silence of origins.

Skyscrapers remind me of my father, houses of my mother.

I never wanted to live too high off the ground. I like to be close to trees and branches. I like not to have to think about falling. I used to borrow a friend's 5th floor penthouse to work in, but the truth is, the balcony being close, I was distracted by the height, could not resist peering over and making up a game of who I could recognize.

*

My first recurring dream of walking occurred when I was five. My great-grandfather, Benno Levy, is walking down a long narrow dirt road with his back to me in a black suit. He's carrying a suitcase. There's dust on his shoes. I want him to turn back. His gait is sturdy, determined. I know he's on his way to his death. (I don't know if he was already dead in "real life.") At his back—the pond in Suffern where I fished for catfish with a string wound around the rabbit's ears of a two-pronged wooden fork. The muddy pond seemed paradisal to me. I would stay outside fishing and chasing the dachshund while the grownups underwent lunch—double-yoked eggs purchased from a nearby chicken farm. I am conscious, from the earliest age, of the need to be outside, not as pure act, but as escape from the tedium, the repetitiveness, of adult life—words exchanged when no words would do.

*

My father and I talked only when we walked because we did not have to face each other. I find it hard to remember my father's springy, relaxed step, his beachy stroll which—consonant with age and terror—degenerated into a shuffle; (to raise the feet is to admit hope for the future). My own gait alongside my father's was always constrained, squeezing myself into the smallest space while he let his elbows swing to and fro. My father was unafraid, unintimidated, would not be squelched. His daytime sobriety was arresting, barrister-like, detached from context.

He never erased the mischievous look of glee and anguish while my features, like my mother's, are strangely stark, angular, and immobile. Physiognomy is fate. The set of the bones in the face. Yet we could still hardly relate—my father's blustery, dramatic surges occupied center stage and made me imagine an upside down world of monologists—Malcom Lowry ordering a "treble gin" after he'd slugged an unwitting dray horse or snapped the mascot rabbit's neck, demanding everyone's attention. I developed a potent weapon: concealment.

*

Once movement is restricted, the walker's view of the city changes irrevocably. I know; I hurt my knee. That year, limping up the subway steps below Lex and 77th, gripping a cane en route to get a surgeon's verdict, I saw a young woman, a flesh-colored skeleton, Hispanic or Indian, jet-black hair, blue jeans, turquoise blue-beaded belt, blue denim shirt, seated on a bench inside the terminus, long fingers pressed flat against the bench as if she were trying to lift herself up, head thrown as far back as it could go, mouth jacked open wide, around an echoing scream, and as I moved on, shoved by the crowd, nervous about falling and further damaging the lining of the joint that had been worn away

by the torn cartilage, I still wanted desperately to help
her. . . . She is frozen there, like a possum on railroad
tracks. Her teeth ground down, ridges of white stumps.
And then her stillness. I looked at her chest. No sign
of breath. No movement.

It was never simple, this matter of my knee, and as I
limped along, encaned, through the throngs, I had a
vision of the future—which had already arrived for so
many I now walked beside—a future unconditionally
tremulous and dim and I was amazed I had not seen
it before.

*

The only other time I walked so slowly was when I
accompanied my blind grandfather on his errands. He
took as much pleasure in his two block trip to Chemical Bank as he might have in an afternoon's walk in
the country. Maybe his blindness didn't bother him as
much as it does others because he had such an acute sense
of smell. He'd been in the perfume business. Colleagues
called him "The Nose." And he was just as proud of
his long wide thick beak as he was of its unseen sen-
sory qualities. He claimed to have invented the de-
odorant, but he took his product (which merely combined his usual scents with hydroxychloride) off the
market because it closed up the pores, interfered with
the sweat glands. He was one of those people who,
having grown up in the country, working with his hands,
hunting, fishing, playing ball, brought a certain pristine vigilance to ecological issues long before they began to be aired in public. He was violently opposed to
aerosol cans and detergents. On one of our long-on-
time, short-on-space walks he railed that he'd been "talking
the detergents for twenty years, but no one listened."

*

Often, in the late afternoons, I would wheel my son in his stroller to the Cathedral of St. John, to see the peacock that we first sighted strutting through the Biblical Herb Garden. (He was hard to see at first with his leafy tail against the bushes.) Once, returning home, we paused by the cathedral's hybrid, baroque Children's Statue, its warlike images of severed heads dangling from claws in opposition to the homage to peace on the plaque. The early moon had risen above the tip of Pegasus' wings; my son reached up and "picked it," putting his hand to his mouth, pretending to chew. But when, a moment later, the moon went behind a cloud and stayed there for what seemed like an eternal instant he burst into tears—"I want my moon back!" He was inconsolable. In the mind of a two-year-old, what's gone is gone forever.

*

Like a psychoanalyst of cities, I try to reconstruct why I find significance in these spaces we traverse, as in a vast red brick building behind an imposing fence on Amsterdam Avenue. It takes up several acres in a city that's always short of space, its sign reads "International Youth Hostelry" and it is the perfect image of our time, I think, an immense empty structure, promising repose and rest, and yet with no possible angle of entry, no real existence beyond its facade. Or, walking through Tompkins Square Park in the gray eerie January rain and afternoon dark, for the first time since the early seventies, to be transported backward in time only to tumble out into another vacant lot strewn with the kind of day it is, the sky hanging its laundry over the yellow rubble. Some neighborhoods in New York look like the outskirts of other cities where everything, suddenly, breaks down. The roofs don't so much cave in as disappear. These inner city outskirts are the parts of the city no one sees, except those who live there, who rarely leave; this is what the imagination needs to reclaim.

*

Much of the pleasure of walking has to do with looking and being unobserved. I don't know how I'd feel about it if I had to think more about being looked at.

Women are never free from this problem. One winter my friend walked into the market square in Isla Mujeres just after 9 in the morning. She was with her daughter, aged three. On their way to find a room for the night, they saw circus trailers, and the little girl asked if they could go to the circus later that night when suddenly two monkeys appeared. One leaped immediately into the girl's arms as if to ravish her, riding on her neck, rubbing his cheek to her cheek. The girl was charmed. The monkey was affectionate but not aggressive. The other monkey leaped onto my friend's back and latched on. At first she thought it was cute but this big spider monkey had tightened his tail around her arm, and she saw her daughter still in the gentle embrace of the other one. The spider monkey tightened his arms around the woman's neck. Panic. She didn't know whether to resist or keep still.

*

In transit for four days, walking, and thinking about the kind of illuminations that might be gathered on the way from here to there; how to make the best of the in between time; about the chiaroscuro of avenues, that moment of iron darkness at dusk; the chance, walking in the city, that you will glimpse someone you haven't seen in ten, maybe twenty years, maybe more, and how that glimpse will take you back.

West Side, Upper West Side, West Village, East Village; I am there, off balance, favoring my left leg by tilting to the right, yet walking, and thinking that great poetry has always been about this—ambulatory movement—and how difficult it is to remember to project ourselves, the unreleased contents of our psyches into, say, that "Abandoned Youth Hostelry." What we choose to see, perceive, is also ourselves. What appears to be chaos is an order of variables. It is the chaos of cities which attracts me.

In the city people are often unsettled by the harsh opposition of extreme wealth and poverty. There is no moment in which these contrasts and tensions do not exist—engendering a furious anomie. The human heart cannot keep pace with a city's changes. (Baudelaire's insight, not mine.)

Walking stirs the broth of the unconscious. A misty labyrinth extends out from our feet. Those terrors about to leap out at us, that free floating libido: they precede what we perceive.

The urban grid levels everything. The idiosyncratic, if we're lucky, can become the essential. What at first seems peripheral may turn out to be central.

*

In the months before my son was born walking had a special cast. Same season as this one: late winter. Plenty of light, little warmth. To get the baby moving my wife and I walked back and forth across Central Park, around the baseball diamonds and the pond below the castle, into and through museums (canvases of bodies embracing, rising and falling and floating at the same time above a dayglo desert further illuminated by the halos of swimming pools . . .), up Broadway to be stared at by many passersby, and then we happened on what looked like a peaceful spot, under some plane trees and away from the rattle of machinery, when a lovely woman with tears in her eyes reached into a yellow phone box to the direct-to-police phone and said, "Miracle! It works!" She wore burgundy cords and an orange cotton turtleneck and held one of her children on her right hip. "There's a little boy lost here. And his mother only speaks Yugoslavian. And his grandmother only speaks Yugoslavian." The next day, retracing our steps to this haven, we run into the woman on Broadway. "The little boy found his way home alone, ten blocks from where he started. And only four years old!"

*

My interest in the physiology of writing may stem from asthma. As a child, unable to listen to the reason of adults, each asthmatic gasp felt like it would be my last. And so to write I felt like I needed a deep breath, and a tremendous head of steam, before I could begin, for fear I'd never get a second wind.

To whatever degree asthma really is brought on by nerves ("stress"!), once you have it you really have something to worry about. The asthmatic lives, cringing inwardly, in fear of suffocation.

Osip Mandelstam and Marcel Proust were asthmatics. This may have made each give priority to breathing, to put breathing in the foreground of consciousness. For Mandelstam, the "rhythm of the human gait" could provide a counterpoint to breathlessness. Proust approached each sentence as if it might have contained his last breath.

*

Walking is one way I have of dealing with my restlessness, and my desire to be far away from here (but where?) right now. These weeks elongate themselves. Even the light grows heavy and leans toward a perpetual evening.

I am much in the mood to get back into a mode where I am again a walker in the city, where what's perceived with each footfall is new and not bound by the conventions of past perception, past connection. But it is difficult to renew oneself endlessly. And yet that is the challenge of poetry (of life!)—to ply contradictions. I am thinking about how some poems mean to teach us about deep physiological rhythms, rhythms that give a poem an almost classical form without strain or archness; stopping, and starting, turning this corner and not that, choosing, and yet not staking everything on each swerve, keeping the next step ahead of the thought, keeping thinking in the body, as an extension of the senses; writing and walking; idle alertness, receptiveness; the need to look outward, (to try), to project fearlessly, to identify and empathize, to arrest the day's (the moment's) flux by writing it down, and drawing strength from that, to trust that what's inside will be implied by the eye-to-object perception, that my sense now as I write of the particulars that surround my life are sufficient to embody vision, that the precise rhythms of these notations are a graph of the spirit. I know that when I remember walking across Tompkins Square Park in the rain the contours of that memory are imbued by the quality of the experience; I was on my way with a friend, or someone congenial, or someone I love. It all shows up, like a watermark. The rain may hurt my head, it may give relief.

The walk becomes metaphorical of the rest of life. There is little that we love to do (or love or do) that is not "fostered *alike*," Wordsworth reminds me, "by beauty and by fear."

Everyone we see becomes a potential doppelgänger (double-goer). The walker in the city becomes the city.

*

As a boy in Chicago I walked the streets in a manic frenzy, surrounded by the immense railroad yard, the military barracks, and—further away but still present to my mind—the stockyards. And everywhere—inescapable—was the prairie. It is possible that my sense of beauty was formed by those contraries. I loved Chicago's mixture of wilderness and civilization. Maybe it mirrored my own restlessness.

*

These bursts of winter light make me restless, uncomfortable with habit, routine, any fixed way of doing things. I'm keyed to a detour. I know that I will vary my daily round. I know that I will wander around the city and kick myself for not having seen so many things before that are right under my nose. And I know that in this state of mind this city (any city?) can become like a foreign country.

In this mood I am impatient with competence, with anything whose result can be in any way predicted. Maybe it's the same impulse that sent Descartes to the wharf in Amsterdam: only among merchants and foreign tongues, the clear give and take of commerce, could he begin to think.

*

My friend and I are walking down West End Avenue in the morning light when we see a man, an albino, standing rigidly upright at the edge of a building but not leaning against it, with his head craned toward the sun, holding a pale lizard in his outstretched palm. We walk past, exchange puzzled glances, and my friend goes back and asks the man what he was doing: "Is that a gekko?" The man responds with pleasure (apparently no one else on their busy way had thought to inquire) and the pride of a messenger whose chance it was to bear good news he had memorized and repeated to himself many times: "They told me to sun it for an hour. Three times a day every three days." He blinked, registering our interest, then began to improvise: "But upstairs . . . upstairs they've got an alligator . . . but he's in the bathtub . . . they don't let me bring him down."

*

I think that walking is the only thing that can cure me (but of what) and only momentarily. I take it back. Walking is the only consuming distraction, in the body, from the body. This is what lures the flaneur to be swallowed up by the crowd.

The rhythm of the swinging swings is not that far removed from walking. The rhythm of walking is not that far removed from the rocking cradle.

Often, walking, I am, for as long as the movement lasts, happy. Walking is a source of immediate joy, life as it is being lived, not contemplated.

Walking, the head stays still, the body moves through space like a flywheel, casting off anything unnecessary. Movement is the key.

Walking, we keep our pact with the earth, more happily than anyone would ever care to admit. Arrested walking brings another kind of perception: static, frightened.

I can tell when the crowd experiences a sudden elevation of mood. I take the pulse of the street and can tell what kind of day it is in the life of our times.

Walking, a slight imbalance (presence of a cumbersome package in one's hand) can turn this heaven into hell.

Hell—a suburb in which no one walks.

Walking puts the eye's prominence back in perspective. It instantiates the self. By identifying changes apart from ourselves we begin to set up internal markers.

Walking needn't be mentioned explicitly. It is the movement of the mind that counts. Merely to think of movement brings happiness.

On Manhattan streets in the violent late January sun— my heart soars.

Walking as embrace. It sets a ground for intimacy, lets

connections occur. We talk and we drift apart. Nothing is demanded. The remembered event provokes the poem, which commemorates the event, marks the passing time, enlivens it, carouses.

Walking tosses up trusted variables. We think we're crossing Central Park but what extends out from us at all sides is a vast empty field that no one else is crossing.

Walking is the lyric of the multitude.

Walking provides a counterpoint, a counterstress, to the solitude of writing. Rising from our reveries, we are loath to be reminded of reality and walking is a gentle immersion.

*

All day I anticipate walking across town, across Central Park, and I know I can merge crossing it with an unimportant but necessary errand. I move erratically, first down Broadway then swerve abruptly left, in a fever to reach the green. This is not a city without havens. I pass a lovely inviting garden, empty in the midday heat, on a block of otherwise uniform, renovated brownstones.

There is nothing you can't walk away, Kierkegaard said, and yes, walking alleviates stress and induces thought—unless you set out on a walk for this purpose, as I did, on a humid afternoon in May, beginning with springy step and great hopes, ending with exhaustion and despair.

I am walking East when I pass the Claremont Stables at 89th and Columbus, where my father rode in the years after he'd given up the luxury of keeping a horse, and where he took me riding when I came to town. This was his central pleasure and luxury, riding every morning before work. In some sense, he never recovered from this loss. What Hildesheimer says of Mozart is also true of my father: "It has also been verified that Mozart went for a horseback ride every morning, beginning in 1787. Dr. Barisani had prescribed riding to compensate for his sedentary life—*probably the only sound advice Mozart ever received in his life*" (my emphasis).

I refresh myself with the dungy smell and the cool shadows. Everything was fine while we rode around in circles in this stable. It's true that my father did ask if I really knew how to ride, and I said, not only that, but I can hold onto the pommel and swing myself from side to side at a gallop. "You mean you ride *Western*?"

Morning at the Dude Ranch. A misty pond and steaming dung. Our group looked like a posse. I couldn't reach the pommel, couldn't get my foot up to the stirrups, so my father hoisted me on. My horse was willing to walk with the others to the end of a trail, but when it broke off into open fields and dilapidated fences, and the other horses broke into a canter, he nuzzled into a weedpatch and commenced an early lunch. I tugged the reins and kicked his flanks. No impact! No response! I was pummelling the girded loins of a frothing indifferent giant. I watched my father, cutting a gallant figure in his black polo shirt and khaki jodhpurs, disappear over a far hill at a gallop—and tugged harder. I beat my fists against the horse's thick impervious neck. I could feel the sound of hooves fading, I did not want to spend the day in the scorching sun, alone, waiting, while the horse sidled from ragweed to goldenrod. The posse had circled back, with red and angry faces. The blood on my palms was pale compared to my humiliation. "C'mon Boy," my father said, clicking his tongue against his palate to get the horse to walk back to the ranch. He looked more comfortable, more at ease in the saddle than I'd ever see him in civilian life.

*

I'm walking past Astor Place toward Gramercy Park in a storm and the harsh light of the crowded street, when a sudden gust collapses my umbrella and I burst out laughing.

I had no desire to find traces of my past on these streets, it went that way against my will: so much of the pleasure of walking is bound up with palpably entering the future, as if that tree moving toward me as I walk were an index of time-in-space. To walk is to feel we are not at the mercy of the instant, that past and present is not flowing through us but that we are flowing through it.

I wonder if we might not consider the unconscious as a spatial construct and think of it as surrounding us.

*

The rain this May morning makes me want to take back everything I've been saying about the pleasure of walking in the city—in *weather*. Only the tops of trees knock about on Broadway, wildly flailing, while there's a stillness at the knees. Heads bowed to keep the rain out of their eyes, people go by, calmly carrying shopping bags, for at that height nothing much is happening, while just above them tree-trunks bend, branches shake, signs rock. The disturbance is all above our heads yet somehow encompassing.

I take it back: this evening, walking along Central
Park West in an infernal mist, the wind blows hard
and steady against my chest, then it stops. Only a faint
spray keeps blowing in my face. To my right, all's serene and quiet. The park looks abandoned but for jog-
gers on the paths and streets that cut across it West to
East. I see no one walking on the grass, or climbing
the sleek black granite rocks. To my left, ambulances,
Hispanic workers clustered beneath umbrellas with signs
around their necks (one reads "Our Mothers Deserve
Better Than This"), silently protesting exploitation by
the Tavern-on-the-Green. At this moment an amber art
deco apartment house, with its striated surface, makes
me think of a ruin, and of how this city—this street—
Central Park West—might appear to a stranger's eye
in a far off time.

*

I am walking behind a couple, each carrying a brief-
case and tucked umbrella. They're walking at a good
clip, at a speed I usually walk, but tonight I'm late
and must walk fast to relieve my wife (who has to go
out at 8) and to give my son his bath and read him
What Do People Do All Day? There are large puddles
on either side of us and it's difficult to pass. As I make
my move to cut ahead the man turns to look at me
and for a second I'm sure it is my college friend, whose
face is unmistakable—hard, carved features, shock of
black hair and high cheekbones like Jack Palance—only
this man's features are softer.

The last time I ran into him in the street we repaired
to his loft in Chelsea. He had, in the two years since

we'd finished school, taken up painting, and the white walls of his loft were strewn with his stark black and white geometric grid paintings.

I next saw him some seven years later at a Christmas party (at which everyone seemed to be turning thirty) in a tropical Soho loft. He was, in every outer sense, unrecognizable in white shirt, blue blazer, gray slacks, Gucci loafers. He had "gone back to school" to become a psychiatric social worker—and that's why, tonight, I think that he could have transformed himself again into the "responsible citizen" on the sidewalk. I would have liked to have seen him tonight, for we shared something—an era.

*

Thinking of Jack Palance makes me remember how he was in Godard's *Contempt*. The movie poster sported Brigitte Bardot's backside in a red towel. My friends and I, out for a night on the town in Scottsdale, Arizona, thought we were going to see a piece of soft porn.

It was a different moon I walked under in the desert that night—broad brimmed. I wasn't looking at the moon now but at the strange mutations in the arroyos and gulleys, the long empty stretches, the scrub grass, the weeds, the sudden dips and bursts of stone. They merged with the crumbling brick walls in the outskirts of Rome in *Contempt*. I was shaken, not ready to engage the disappointed faces of my friends who weren't even granted full erections. I stupidly confessed how much I had liked the movie and so let myself open to a chorus of jeers and hoots.

After *Contempt*, I walked past the vacant lot where Sheila and I had taken refuge in the dark, under the open sky, after the restaurant proprietess with a rich Italian accent herded us off the bathroom floor, screaming, "What are you doing in there together? This is not a house of prostitution."

I realized now that I had never seen this space before: in the eerie, gray and white light, this junkyard had the magnificent shocked grandeur of a ruin.

*

We wake in the dark, in pleasure, in the rain, and I anticipate walking later under the blowing trees. My son's silhouetted in the doorway, in his Tweety pajamas, rubbing his eyes, muttering, in his gruff voice: "You go to sleep in the dark, and you wake up in the dark."

*

Greenwich Avenue/*Peacock Café*. It is always around noon when I reach Greenwich Avenue, walking east. I pass the schoolyard where it's always recess, I look up and see the children's paintings on the back of a building, lined up, framed, to look like windows. I can feel myself gather momentum, as if the wind were at my back. It's as if the day were turning on its axis, its axle, at this moment; the light is changing to darkness now even though it will be slow to arrive. I can use the morning; the afternoon uses me.

Once, several years ago, I ducked into the Peacock to finish preparing for a class I had never taught before. A woman I once knew was at the next table, deep in conversation with a nun. She paused at my table on her way out. "I live in a monastery now," she said. "I'm becoming a priest." Then, with relief and a slight grin: "I've taken a vow of celibacy." I couldn't think of anything to say. "You look nervous," she said. I stared down at the chaos of my lecture notes. "I have a lot to do before class," I said. "I can see that," she said. And as she walked away I had no clear sense of whether she seemed better off now or worse.

*

"Sometimes," (my son prefaces everything with that phrase), we exit the park and walk by The Dakota— 72nd and Central Park West. He's always taken with the urge to smite the fetching gargoyles whose faces are at his eye level along the railing. While he's absorbed in that drama I imagine that I am in a medieval town somewhere in Provence, surrounded by magpies and the stern, contorted faces of the gargoyles. From this imagined hilltop I can see mushrooming shapes and colors, pale olives, soft blues and grays. Wasps cluster at the honey jars on the stone tables on the terrace but no one brushes them away. No one gets stung. "They're not gargoyles—they're monsters!" He shouts and jolts me back to where I am.

I feel as if I'm most flaneur-like when we're walking at a turtle's pace he sets. It brings to mind Antony's marvelous address to Cleopatra:

> No Messenger but thine, and all alone to night
> We'll wander through the streets, and note
> The qualities of people.

He must sample every hawker's tray for cars and trucks and guns, must yank every stray cord out of the tarred

dirt, walk every catwalk, jump on or over every grat-
ing, every manhole. I don't like to think of what could
happen if one were loose. "Stop it," I say. "But I *like*
to," he says. I tell him about the eight-year-old who
stepped on a loose manhole cover, fell under the earth,
got sucked down, drowned. "Where were his mommy
and his daddy?" he asks, as if by their mere presence
they could have saved him from harm. "Daddy." "What,
Sam." "What's *drowned*?"

*

Walking upper Broadway's dire grid in the raw February air after a late Friday afternoon movie (*Three
Fugitives*) my son lurches to each corner, then comes
to an abrupt stop, hops around to face me, and waits.
Two blocks from our apartment he wants to know if
this is "New York?" His most constant refrain since
he first formed words has been: "Where we go-ing?"
Which is always germane. "Where's that man going?"
Or where the clouds have gone, why the wind blew
them away, or why they're hiding under the park bench.

There is a man sitting on a garbage can, strumming a
three-stringed, half-gutted guitar. Lean and handsome,
he wears heavy green woolen army pants. My son asks,
"Can I strum? Why it's only got half a face?" The man
laughs, gently, and hands it to him with one word of
caution: "Be careful, it's very delicate."

*

There are no longer many places where walking deliv-
ers joy. Most people have a constant pattern, in which
there are not enough variables. Rhythm imitates bodily
contexts. Whitman's easy gait is the mother of his prosody.

Only by picturing him as part of a multitude can we grasp how easily his "I" becomes mine, or yours. Whitman's call to the open road has a formal component, a structure.

Walking icy roads in Vermont, I was forced to shuffle and keep my body on an even keel. Then, in a burst of bravado, I failed—and fell. Only the streets of Manhattan are second nature to me. There I can move at breakneck speed, never stopping, dancing through traffic, never once stopping for a light. The entire pleasure of living in the city is tied up with walking.

*

No, days are not marked on the calendar, linear time can do no more than corroborate effects, but there is a certain mustiness like an illness that has to be overthrown before we can begin.

And so it is no accident that I write on this, the first clement day of the year, to gain clemency. I could consider the mustiness my own, but what light alleviates is no one's property.

Language describes a possibility and it is possible to be myself once I give up the need for unity, consistency. The lights (they were not desperate) on the river under the bridge, are city lights, and yet the moment seems pristine, almost pastoral.

The word, if it contained the world, would tell all.

*

"You're Little John. I'm Robin."
"Ok, Rob."

"Come on, Little John, there's bad guys under the tree!"
"Ok, Rob, let's go get them!"
"Robin's an actor. What's his name?"

"Erroll Flynn," my wife answers. I hold back from telling
them what I glimpsed (guilty for watching it at all as
a ritual way of easing in to work) on *Geraldo* this morning,
and how violently I reacted. . . . Erroll Flynn's stunt
double, Buster Wiles, was on to clear Flynn of all charges
for posterity. I was with him at all times, he says, and
I can guarantee he wasn't gay, wasn't a Nazi spy, never
laid a hand on that girl. Her father was the child mo-
lester and he blackmailed Flynn. The tremor in Buster
Wiles' hand is a shocking admission. Involuntarily he
draws his cane again and again across his sunken chest.
His twitching shakes me more than my stepfather's
ever did in real life, even after he was diagnosed, wrongly,
as having Parkinson's.

Having recently buried my father, and knowing that
my stepfather is (even without Parkinson's) feeble, I
have become vulnerable to the sufferings of the anonymous
old, strangers who cross my path and pass on. I watch
an old couple walk a narrow dirt path above where
we are playing catch, each footstep as deliberate as a
tightrope walker's.

*

My son and I watched *The Adventures of Robin Hood*
the weekend of his fourth birthday. He seemed suspicious as Robin pulled arrow after arrow out of his slender
quiver in the scene where he was trapped alone in the
castle with all the prince's men after him. "Why Robin's

got so many arrows?" The Robin he knew before was
a cartoon fox with greater limitations. Greater reserve.

*

The actors I read about these days are their own stunt
doubles.

Every man his own doppelgänger.

*

We walk the jogging trail home through Riverside Park,
my son stumbling and falling as he tries to munch a
bagel and carry his bow and three arrows in the other
hand. It's the kind of perfect hour in the light with the
wind off the river that it is impossible to transcend.
The vanishing instant cuts acutely across our eyebrows.
His sense of being at odds is entirely bound up with
objects: bagel, bow, arrow, quiver to be made at home,
the hat my wife fashioned out of newspaper, the tights
she donated to his costume (and miraculously fit him).
It is we who are left guessing, and come up short; we
who must be content that knowing always remains at
a distance, disappearing: the gap is binding.

*

Walking, I watch the plastic baggie wafting on the wind,
I follow its shadow on the avenue, I see it snagged by
a branch and released, I wonder from what height it
has fallen, if it was thrown out intentionally or was
sucked out by the wind by an open window; I want to
lie back, and drift and dream and listen to the spare
Brazilian guitar; I want to lie with my head again on
her lap in Kensington Square Park; I want to lie down
on the lawn in Kankakee, under the maple tree, some

spring afternoon after school, thinking of no before or after, and wait, anxiously or not anxiously, for the little band to come by and play wiffle ball; or to lie prone on the grass in Paterson, New York, after work, in the early spring sun, knowing I would be alone and free the rest of the day. In the late afternoons you can hide in broad daylight. I want concord, concordance, with what the self inside the self is trying to be, manifest energy, as in those times when no one was pulling me apart, when routines were suspended, and I was with friends who granted my wish to be normal, saw me as I wanted to be seen, and not—as my father saw me— as a victim of circumstances; or as when I knew almost no one in New York and walked the hundred blocks from my apartment to hers, drinking cheap Portugese wine, and reeling.

*

Later, moving west alone across Central Park at 79th, I walk out of the Vista Rock Tunnel into a burst of noonday light, not carrying anything, not going anywhere in particular—a rush of radiance, a haze on bush and branch—the rain stops falling and I walk the city in the sun; I breathe easy as the light presses against the stand of trees on the rise above old stone walls. . . . Ready to begin again.

ON TRANSLATION:
DOSTOYEVSKY AND HOMER IN ENGLISH

We approach translations with great expectations. Translation is a way of incorporating, without necessarily colonizing, the experience of other cultures. It is also an act of essential criticism: the translator must decide to preserve certain elements and eliminate others. The task for translators is to stick to their decisions. Languages are, after all, incommensurable, which is why there are so many kinds of translations. In "The Task of the Translator," Walter Benjamin singles out the French and German words for bread, "pain" and "brod," to reveal the unhealable (and tormenting to the translator) rupture between words and, ultimately, between worlds.

What are the classic translations? In addition to George Chapman's Homer and Pope's Homer I would include Arthur Golding's *Metamorphoses*, Sir Thomas Urquart and Peter Anthony Motteux's Rabelais, Thomas Hobbes' Thucydides, Tobias Smollett's *Don Quixote*, Constance Garnett's Chekhov, Ezra Pound's *Cathay* and *Confucian Odes*, Marianne Moore's *The Fables of La Fontaine*, Richard Wilbur's Molière, William Arrowsmith's *Satyricon*, W.S. Merwin's *Song of Roland*, Ralph Manheim's *Journey to the End of Night*, M.L. Rosenthal's *Pinocchio* and, recently, David Slavitt's *Ovid's Poetry of Exile*. Now, two highly acclaimed versions of classics have appeared with an attempt on the parts of both publishers to take over the market, which means replacing previous versions in the classroom. Let us see how well they fulfill their claims.

The Brothers Karamazov, translated by Richard Pevear and Larissa Volokhonsky, and *The Iliad*, translated by Robert Fagles, bring together many of the problems of translating prose and poetry.

Read in tandem, the works reveal unforeseeable affinities. The role of mind in *The Iliad* and *The Brothers Karamazov* is strikingly similar, given the 2,500 years that separated the authors: in some fundamental way that goes beyond character and theme, both books are about acting out commands. In *The Iliad* the gods give the orders; in *The Brothers Karamazov* the unconscious does, with similar force, through compulsions and obsessive thinking. The role of Achilles and the role of Dimitri (Mitya) Karamazov isn't that different: both are military men; both are waiting to act out their fate; both are chafing at delay; both have been put on hold, in some sense infantilized. (Achilles sulks and Mitya becomes hysterical.) Achilles wants his consort, Briseis, whom Agamemnon has denied him; Mitya wants the money due him from his mother's estate and he wants Grushenka, whom his father is also courting. Both must wait. The stories take place in the hell of that caesura.

Another parallel between *The Iliad* and *The Brothers Karamazov* offers itself: the central transformation of the heroes is tied up to reconciliation with the father. In Achilles' case, it is not his own father, but Priam, Hector's father, who is the vehicle for the great change that comes over him, makes him human and, tragically, concurrently, gets him ready to die the death he has long rehearsed—the death he knows will gain him immortality.

"Revere the gods, Achilles! Pity me in my own right,
remember your own father! I deserve more pity . . .
I have endured what no one on earth has ever done
    before—
I put to my lips the hands of the man who killed my
    son."

Those words stirred within Achilles a deep desire
to grieve for his own father. Taking the old man's
    hand
he gently moved him back. And overpowered by
    memory
both men gave way to grief. Priam wept freely
for man-killing Hector, throbbing, crouching
before Achilles' feet as Achilles wept himself,
now for his father, now for Patroclus once again,
and their sobbing rose and fell throughout the house.

Achilles' heroic stature is never in question; Mitya
Karamazov becomes an exemplary sufferer only after
he goes through the trial of his father's death. Achilles
will be released into death any day now: there he can
remain a hero. Mitya will have to wrestle with his compulsions
every day of his life. In neither Homer nor Dostoyevsky
are there palliatives to suffering.

*

No writer can become more indelibly stamped on
our early years than Dostoyevsky. I first read *The Brothers
Karamazov* as a raw youth, going from the book to the
coffee shop or bar where the same kind of conversa-
tions were going on all the time—when all we did was
talk, day and night, about Dostoyevsky and Kierkegaard
and their twentieth-century counterparts.

I first read the book on several warm spring afternoons on the tarred roof of a friend's house in Brooklyn, fending off droves of neighborhood cats that she fed. And I could tell who among my friends were also reading it—their wicked ("pale and crooked") grins showed me. Ivan was our man; for we mistook the explicit philosophizing of the book for its meaning. (We were in good company. D.H. Lawrence found Ivan "the greatest of the three brothers, pivotal.") It may be absurd to think of Ivan as a mouthpiece for the author—as we were encouraged to do by the inclusion of "The Grand Inquisitor" in anthologies of existentialism—but it would be equally absurd to propose that Dostoyevsky did not intend Ivan's vision as a distinct possibility in a world of possibility. The most chilling parts of the book are Ivan's encounters with his two very different "doubles," Smerdyakov and "The Devil," because they echo his own sentiments back to him. His words, uttered in their different spirit, are utterly changed. And these grotesque, distorted figures in some way anticipate the reader who goes away from the book wide-eyed and dishevelled saying, "Everything is permitted."

Most English and American readers have first encountered Dostoyevsky (and Turgenev, and Tolstoy, and Chekhov) in Constance Garnett's translations. In 1912, according to Frank Swinnerton's account, "every young literary or pseudo-literary person in London seized and consumed with a fury of delight the first complete translations, made by Constance Garnett, of Dostoyevsky's *The Brothers Karamazov*. It was declared the greatest novel ever written." Freud concurred. And it was the one book Wittgenstein took with him to the front in 1917.

But Constance Garnett, in her desire to make Dostoyevsky immediately accessible, flattened his tone. She trans-

lates Mitya's "wild speech" as something to be stated
rather than declaimed.

> Though I sit alone in a pillar—I exist! I see the sun,
> and if I don't see the sun, I know it's there. And
> there's a whole life in that, in knowing that the sun
> is there.

Besides creating a confused metaphor of "sit alone in
a pillar," (was she trying to suggest "pillory"?), she
holds something back here: the effect is muted, played
down. Her light touch is tonally right for Chekhov and
Turgenev, but not for Dostoyevsky's volcanic imagination. Her version is too "correct" to convey the full
weight of compulsion in Dostoyevsky, much less his
convulsive style. Pevear and Volokhonsky are able to
translate with such firmness because they have grasped
one of Dostoyevsky's crucial insights: that it is not
through thought but through action that the characters undergo their great changes and come to know
themselves. Eccentricity, in their version, is a symp-
tom of the characters' distance from God.

Richard Pevear, a poet and translator of Alain, Yves
Bonnefoy, Alberto Savinio, from French and Italian,
has collaborated with Larissa Volokhonsky, a Russian
emigré, to produce this version. Pevear and Volokhonsky
bring a knotty complexity to Dostoyevsky's lines which
we register almost subliminally, as we do the rhythms
of good English prose. Take this passage, where Madame Khokhalakov is talking about her daughter Lise:

> "Recently, for instance, talking about a pine tree: there
> was a pine tree standing in our garden when she
> was very little, maybe it's still standing, so there's
> no need to speak in the past tense. Pines are not people,

Alexei Fyodorovich, they take a long time to change. 'Mama,' she said, 'how I pine for that pine'—you see, 'pine' and 'pine'—but she put it some other way, because something's confused here, pine is such a silly word, only she said something so original on the subject that I decidedly cannot begin to repeat it. Besides, I've forgotten it all."

Here is Constance Garnett's translation:

"She spoke lately about a pine-tree, for instance: there used to be a pine-tree standing in our garden in her early childhood. Very likely it's standing there still; so there's no need to speak in the past tense. Pine-trees are not like people, Alexey Fyodorovitch, they don't change quickly. 'Mamma,' she said, 'I remember this pine-tree as in a dream,' only she said something so original about it that I can't repeat it. Besides, I've forgotten it."

Madame Khokhalakov's wacky, muddled remembrance is a good instance of how Dostoyevsky uses particularized speech patterns to indicate who is talking. You begin to think *you're* dreaming when, comparing the two translations, you find something like "as in a dream" when there is no dream in the "pine . . . pine" translation. But when you discover that the homophones Dostoyevsky uses, *sosna* and *sos-na*, translates as both "pine-tree" *and* "dream" it begins to make sense. Garnett, with "as in a dream," decided to sacrifice the mild pun on pine. She seeks to avoid distracting the reader at a moment when the speaker's distractedness, the yearning within the recollection, is precisely the point. Pevear and Volokhonsky's version is both more immediate and more ambiguous, more familiar and more

alien. The repetition of "pine" lets the strangeness remain strange. So much of translation is a matter of
tact rather than literal rightness.

This non-grammar, or disordered order of perceptions, which Garnett generously "corrected," is important to the construction of *The Brothers Karamazov*. It
reflects the consciousness of the characters under stress:
the thoughts of Ivan and Alyosha running into each
other like inlet and ocean; Mitya watching Feodor
Karamazov's Adam's apple bob and snatching the brass
pestle from his pocket as he *thinks* of murdering him:
"The whole of the old man's profile, which he found
so loathsome, the whole of his drooping Adam's apple,
his hooked nose, smiling in sweet expectation, his lips—
all was brightly lit from the left by the slanting light
of the lamp shining from the room."

Normally we see a smile on the lips—but not in *The
Brothers Karamazov*. To mirror Mitya's deranged state
of mind at that moment, Dostoyevsky transposes "the
old man's lips" and his smile. Garnett homogenizes
the sentences, makes it sound like a more normal order of perceptions. "The old man's profile that he loathed
so, his pendant Adam's apple, his hooked nose, his
lips that smiled in greedy expectation, were all brightly
lighted up by the slanting lamplight falling on the left
from the room."

The Brothers Karamazov is a carnal comedy. The narrator is telling the story of the Karamazovs under compulsion: he's perverse, impatient; he gets ahead of himself,
and behind (he waits until the end of the book to tell
us the name of the town). In a departure from Constance
Garnett's 1912 translation, Pevear and Volokhonsky have
restored the narrator's complex, outrageous, at times

hysterical voice. This narrator, far from seeking the Flaubertian ideal of the right word, finds that no one word will do the trick: he is always hemming and hawing, clearing his throat, waffling, choosing to tell one thing or another on the spur of the moment.

> But it was not yet three o'clock in the afternoon when something occurred that I have already mentioned at the end of the previous book, something so little expected by any of us, and so contrary to the general hope, that, I repeat, a detailed and frivolous account of this occurrence has been remembered with great vividness in our town and all the neighborhood even to the present day. Here again I will add, speaking for myself personally, that I find it almost loathsome to recall this frivolous and tempting occurrence, essentially quite insignificant and natural, and I would, of course, omit all mention of it from my story, if it had not influenced in the strongest and most definite way the soul and heart of the main, *though future*, hero of my story, Alyosha . . .

Pevear and Volokhonsky have perceived the comic potential of his pedantry, his distractedness, his throat-clearing, strung with qualifiers like "as if" and "as it were." Dostoyevsky is after an effect that is closer to the dialogues of Plato and Diderot and Leopardi (in *The Moral Essays*) than to the novels of Flaubert and Turgenev and James, all of whom are notably "visual" writers.

Dostoyevsky's insistence on a direct line to the spirit—no need for exact words, precise descriptions—provoked the ire of Nabokov, who once gleefully quoted Turgenev's remark that Dostoyevsky was a "new pimple on the nose of Russian literature." Though a murder is at the heart of all of Dostoyevsky's four major novels, there is something disingenuous about Nabokov's assertion that *The Brothers Karamazov,* his culminating master-piece, is a "typical detective story," (though this may be no worse than taking it for a philosophical or reli-gious tract, or a *tragedy* of parricide, as Freud did).

Perhaps Nabokov disliked Dostoyevsky because he was denying an influence. It could be said that all of Nabokov comes out of Dostoyevsky's *The Double*—though Nabokov's mad characters, with their doubles, are more frighten-ingly detached than Dostoyevsky's tormented souls. Dostoyevsky's descriptions are stark outlines, charcoal sketches across the surface. It is not, as Nabokov claims, that "the weather does not exist in his world," but that Dostoyevsky's characters, though consumed by their in-ner thoughts, are always rushing somewhere, and their physical world reflects this movement. Even in a dream,

> it seems to Mitya that he is cold, it is the beginning of November, and snow is pouring down in big, wet flakes that melt as soon as they touch the ground. And the peasant is driving briskly, waving his whip nicely, he has a long, fair beard, and he is not an old man, maybe around fifty, dressed in a gray peasant coat. And there is a village nearby—black, black huts, and half of the huts are burnt, just charred beams sticking up.

Dostoyevsky's novels never resolve into a single theme or chord. The Russian critic Mikhail Bakhtin, in his ground breaking study of Dostoyevsky, maintains that the plurality of voices in Dostoyevsky's "polyphonic" novels, in which every word has its shadow, or double, constitutes the ulimate chorus which comprises Dostoyevsky's "poetics." It is these poetics (Dostoyevsky referred to his novels as *poemas*) that are most difficult to access in previous translations. In *The Brothers Karamazov* the main characters are ruffled by contradiction. Because they cannot escape their own natures, they are driven to act—even, perhaps, to kill. Dostoyevsky's characters burn with a fervor for a unitary truth which is in direct opposition to what I take to be Dostoyevsky's attitude as an artist. Part of his gift lay in perceiving the potentially endless permutations of his characters' impossible quests. Dostoyevsky seems to have worked these polarities out of his system by giving them full rein, making them the substance of his art. Ivan breaks his mind against the idea that the suffering of children makes life intolerable: Mitya is fixated on his father's baseness. They are kept from parricide by modern gods— guilt, conscience. There is a reason why Ivan's proclamations are mocked by Smerdyakov and the Devil: they shadow him, as it were, because he refuses to recognize his own culpability. By the time the Devil has had his day you hardly know who's who among the four brothers, Mitya, Ivan, Smerdyakov, even Alyosha. The characters' thoughts are somehow collective, part of a larger community. They hear within themselves what they imagine others to be thinking; their thoughts are continually anticipated, echoed, or reflected in what others are about to say.

"I know only one thing," Alyosha said, still in the same near whisper. "It was not *you* who killed father."

"'Not you'! What do you mean by 'not you'?" Ivan was dumbfounded.

"It was not you who killed father, not you!" Alyosha repeated firmly.

The silence lasted for about half a minute.

"But I know very well it was not me—are you raving?" Ivan said with a pale and crooked grin. His eyes were fastened, as it were, on Alyosha. The two were again standing under a streetlight.

"No, Ivan, you've told yourself several times that you were the murderer."

"When did I . . . ? I was in Moscow [when the murder occurred] . . . When did I say so?" Ivan stammered, completely at a loss.

"You've said it to yourself many times while you were alone during these two horrible months," Alyosha continued as softly and distinctly as before. But he was speaking not of himself, as it were, not of his own will, but obeying some irresistible command. "You've accused yourself and confessed to yourself that you and you alone are the murderer. But it was not you who killed him, you are mistaken, the murderer was not you, do you hear, it was not you. God has sent me to tell you that."

It is Dostoyevsky's genius to bring this vulnerable state, where the boundary between the self and others is diminished, into the light of day. He *sustains* the presence of the uncanny.

Mitya's fixation on money, which he needs and deserves, becomes a comic trope. "And to think that a man's fate should be ruined because of a worthless three thousand roubles!" This echolalia of "roubles" breaks down the reader's resistance. Is he going to talk about roubles, the money owed him, *again*? These roubles become a kind of false answer to problems of deeper deprivations, which are never quite revealed in the novel, except that Mitya also becomes obsessed, through "the wee ones," with the intolerability of children's suffering; the roubles become the substitute for every deprivation of his own childhood—for that which is owed him and can never be repaid. It is this omission of the deeper source of troubles in the Karamazovs' childhoods which gives the novel its terrific centrifugal force. They have no defenses, and are driven into a frenzy because they perceive too keenly the accidental nature of their existence.

Faith is at the heart of it. The novel's epigraph makes clear that *The Brothers Karamazov* is in many ways a work about faith and grace:

> Verily, verily, I say unto you, except a corn of wheat fall into the ground and die, it abideth alone: but if it die, it bringeth forth much fruit. (John 12:24)

And translators must be willing to make the leap to clarify these matters, if they want to make the novel live in another language.

When Mitya, utterly transformed in the process of his incarceration, even though he is not guilty, bursts forth in his "wild speech" (accompanied by breathlessness, trembling, and tears) Pevear and Volokhonsky convey the great change that has taken place within him by the use of manic emphases—itself a leap of faith in the rightness of their decision.

> And it seems to me there's so much strength in me now that I can overcome everything, all sufferings, only in order to say and tell myself every moment: I am! In a thousand torments—I am; writing under torture—but I am. Locked up in a tower, but still I exist, I see the sun, and if I don't see the sun, still I know it is. And the whole of life is there—in knowing that the sun *is*.

Perhaps it is only now, with the benefit of other translations and seventy years of Dostoyevsky scholarship, that it is possible for Pevear and Volokhonsky to convey what we always sensed was *The Brothers Karamazov*: its Russianness, its difference—the issues of grace, soul, faith, love, which are not exactly the standard repertory of the English novel.

While translators of Homer have had formal poetic models for the kind of translations they want to effect, Pevear and Volokhonsky had to listen entirely to the signals of the Russian text and evolve a kind of English of which there are only intimations in existing works. We can now register the full impact of this work, enough to value it as highly as anything written in our own language. And readers who put down *The Brothers Karamazov* shaken, reawakened, as they should be, will find their own feelings clarified, highlighted by this new version. The disturbance that we perceive in the souls of the Karamazovs is also in the surface of the language—that is, at the level of style, at which literature exists. *What sort of people can there be after this?*

*

Each translation of Homer reflects its own time. Though Pope's *Iliad* is the most complete poetic adaptation of Homer's epic in its own right we are likely to have in English, his heroic couplets are a far cry from Homer's unrhymed, rugged hexameters. His powerfully "Englished" version, to which the British eagerly subscribed, must have confirmed their sense of England's supremacy. It remained for Richmond Lattimore to restore Homer's Greekness, in his version, first published in 1951. Those who were reared on his *Iliad* stand by it fiercely. And why not? No one has better rendered in English the beat of Homer's hexameter, which is to Greek verse what the Alexandrine is to French and blank verse is to English.

> Sing, goddess, the anger of Peleus' son Achilleus
> and its devastation, which put pains thousandfold
>   upon the Achaians,
> hurled in their multitudes to the house of Hades
>   strong souls
> of heroes, but gave their bodies to be the delicate
>   feasting
> of dogs, of all birds, and the will of Zeus was
>   accomplished
> since that time when first there stood in division of
>   conflict
> Atreus' son the lord of men and brilliant Achilleus.

Lattimore's version is something of a tour de force, a unique poetic document that will probably "last." But the frequently awkward syntax ("since that time when first there stood") makes it treacherously free of any discourse with the poetic diction of its time.

While choosing in 1951, out of deference to Lattimore's *Iliad*, to approach Homer through *The Odyssey*, Robert Fitzgerald, a skilled poet with a fine ear, turned back to *The Iliad* after some twenty years, possibly because he felt the need to compensate for Lattimore's remoteness from English rhythm and syntax. He set out to make a poem in English that would exploit the "full orchestra" of the language. Translation allowed him to reach for an ideal of language, an absolute music, a certain pitch of blank verse that flows from Milton to Wordsworth and on to Keats and Eliot. Translating *The Iliad* into gorgeous language like this—

>   or a field
> of standing grain when the wind-puffs from the west
> cross it in billows, and the tasseled ears
> are bent and tossed:

gave Fitzgerald the chance to echo the music he heard in a line like Keats' "Thy hair soft-lifted by the winnowing wind" in "To Autumn." What in his own poems might have been seen as derivative lives in a translation.

In his supple blank verse Fitzgerald puts us where the poem is—on that last beach below Troy's towers in the blazing light and lash of waves where the tall ships are moored. Sound does the work: we hear, almost subliminally, a spear being withdrawn from a belly, or another body thudding to the ground. To keep the narrative moving, he skillfully deletes many of the epithets that probably served a purpose when *The Iliad* was an oral poem, but now clog the text.

> Meriones
> went after him and hit him with a spear-throw
> low between genitals and navel, there
> where pain of war grieves mortal wretches most.
> The spear transfixed him. Doubled up on it,
> as a wild bullock in the hills will writhe
> and twitch when herdsmen fetter and drag him
> down,
> so did the stricken man—but not for long
> before Meriones bent near and pulled out
> spearhead from flesh. Then night closed on his eyes.

There is great power in Fitzgerald's restraint and understatement.

Sometimes translations refer not to the poetic idiom of the day but to that of a generation just before. Now that modernism has been fully assimilated into the mainstream of poetic culture, translators like Fitzgerald and Logue are free to proceed in what has become, in its own way, a classic mode. Robert Fagles has clearly set out to do an *Iliad* that would be more colloquial than Lattimore's, harsher than Fitzgerald's. This handsome edition contains a fine seventy-five page introduction by the renowned classicist Bernard Knox and includes copious notes, such as are conspicuously missing from Lattimore's and Fitzgerald's versions.

Robert Fagles is a classicist and prolific translator whose previous works include a vigorous version of Aeschylus' *Oresteia*. And, while the Fagles energetic *Iliad* is quite "readable," I would hesitate to call it a poem. There seems to me a distortion in the way Fagles has allegorized Homer at every turn. By line forty of the poem he has anthropomorphized the waves in a heavy-handed attempt at foreshadowing, suggesting that nature mirrors the human conflict, but there is no indication in the other translations that this should be the case:

> The old man was terrified. He obeyed the order,
> turning, trailing away in silence down the shore
> where the roaring battle lines of breakers crash and
> drag.

Here is Fitzgerald's version:

> So harsh he was, the old man feared and obeyed him,
> in silence trailing away
> by the shore of the tumbling clamorous whispering
> sea.

And Lattimore's:

> So he spoke, and the old man in terror obeyed him
> and went silently away beside the murmuring sea
> beach.

Since war permeates every breath in *The Iliad* it is hardly necessary to anthropomorphize the waves in just this way. Fitzgerald's approximations here, "tumbling clamorous whispering sea" of *poluphloisboio thalassas,* Homer's frequent onomatopoetic expression for the sea's many voices and the waves' rise and fall, is more reflective of Homer's music. And Lattimore's "murmuring sea beach" has its own stark dignity.

Men wage war because they cannot wait for death. *The Iliad* is already an abattoir; Fagles trumpets war as harshly and brashly as he can. His decision is clearly to pump up the violence, make it more graphic, as in the night raid of Odysseus and Diomedes on the Trojan camp.

> Athena, eyes blazing,
> breathed fury in Diomedes and he went whirling
> into the slaughter now, hacking left and right
> and hideous groans broke from the dying Thracians
> slashed by the sword—the ground ran red with
> blood.
>
> *
>
> By now the son of Tydeus came upon the king,
> the thirteenth man, and ripped away his life,
> his sweet life as he lay there breathing hard.
> A nightmare hovered above his head that night—
> Diomedes himself!

Fagles uses these shock effects to underscore what is already implicit in the action—the equivalent of a soundtrack's ominous music. Fitzgerald's recumbent Trojan may be dreaming of his own death when he meets it, but maybe not.

> At last
>
> when Diomedes reached the Thracian king,
> he took a thirteenth precious life away
> as the man gasped in sleep, nightmare upon him.

This kind of subjectivity, this reading into inner life, is alien to Homer. For Homer, nightmares, panic and terror are still external forces, or apparitions sent from the Gods.

Fagles pads the text with unnecessary details, strews it with extra words and syllables. He seems torn between his decision to make his version colloquial and still keep the hexameter (to which English is so inhospitable), and his decision to keep many of the ubiquitous epithets and repetitions. He can decide to translate all of the epithets or none or some, but if he chooses the last he must be available at all times to the impulse of the text. This is not a matter of correctness or fidelity to the original: it is a matter of tone.

> So they fought to the death around the benched
>   beaked ship
> as Patroclus reached Achilles, his great commander,
> and wept warm tears like a dark spring running
>   down
> some desolate rock face, its shade currents flowing.
> And the brilliant runner Achilles saw it coming,
> filled with pity and spoke out winging words

What effect, finally, is he after? The tone wavers uncertainly between high style and plain style. I'm all for his idiomatic *"some* desolate rock face," with its nod to William Carlos Williams' phrasing in "To Elsie":

> sent out at fifteen to work in
> some hard-pressed
> house in the suburbs—
>
> some doctor's family, some Elsie—

This is a perfectly appropriate appropriation for a translator. But then he upsets that colloquial tone when "shade currents" ushers in its romantic/symbolist horde of associations. He further sabotages his own effort by dragging in the pedestrian epithets, *"brilliant* runner Achilles," the sappy *"filled* with pity," and, finally, the inapt *"winging words,"* which falls like lead on the ear. The adjectives diminish the power of the nouns.

Fitzgerald preserves the spontaneous, involuntary nature of grief and conveys Achilles' tautness through his quick rhythm, the muscle-contracting, consonantal, "Achilles watched him come," where Fagles merely alludes to his rank and prowess—"great commander," "brilliant runner."

> That was the way the fighting went
> for one seagoing ship. Meanwhile Patroklos
> approached Akhilleus his commander, streaming
> warm tears—like a shaded mountain spring
> that makes a rockledge run with dusky water.
> Akhilleus watched him come, and felt a pang for him.
> Then the great prince and runner said:
>   "Patroklos,
> why all the weeping?

Though "dusky" is a well-tried part of Fitzgerald's glossary, it brings with it associations (Milton's "Midnight brought on the duskie houre/Friendliest to sleep and silence," Scott's "dusky apartments," and Henry

and silence," Scott's "dusky apartments," and Henry
James's epithet for Nathaniel Hawthorne's work) that
may be almost too splendid, too lush, too determined,
for this context. A word's history never quiets down.
The translator must be able to think ahead, and predict its echoes.

Before Fitzgerald undertook to translate *The Iliad*, the
English poet Christopher Logue was at work on an
adaptation of books 16, 17, 18, *Patrocleia of Homer*, not
published here until 1988, as *War Music*—which begins with Patroclus donning Achilles' armor and going into battle.

Logue's *War Music* is an imitation, a poem launched
by Homer's words. His language is stripped down, taut
as a bowstring, but fully resonant. Logue—"unencum-
bered by Greek scholarship," his collaborator the inspired classicist D.S. Carne-Ross puts it—can take a
particularly untranslatable passage from the Greek—
the shout signalling Achilles' return to battle, and serve
its terror and rage with a full-throated cry that shivers
the Trojan camp.

> Achilles on the rampart by the ditch:
> He lifts his face to ninety; draws his breath;
> And from the bottom of his heart emits
> So long and loud and terrible a scream,
> The icy scabs at either end of earth
> Winced in their sleep; and in the heads that fought
> It seemed as if, and through his voice alone,
> The whole world's woe could be abandoned to the
>   sky.

Logue's approach is both lyric and cinematic. Like
Fitzgerald, he cuts out the epic's epithets and repetitions,
but he also brings in details from contemporary life.

> Consider planes at touchdown—how they poise;
> Or palms beneath a numbered hurricane;
> Or birds wheeled sideways over windswept heights;
> Or burly salmon challenging a weir;
> Right-angled, dreamy fliers, as they ride
> The instep of a dying wave, or trace
> Diagonals on snowslopes

This is a Homer without compromises. Logue opts for lyric intensity over narrative flow and continuity. With help from Carne-Ross (whose afterword to *Patrocleia* constitutes its own challenge to translators "in the belief that no sort of fancy translationese should be allowed to muffle the impact of the original"), Logue mediates between the Greek and the English. He has reduced the number of actual lines by two-thirds, but the effect of the sequence is enlarged, given added torque.

Logue's is a modernist Homer, a Homer on high-contrast paper. He does to Homer what Pound did to Eliot's early version of *The Waste Land*: he retains only those verbal clusters whose energy is most intense. Logue sacrifices narrative in order to complement the stark, elemental beauty of the Trojan shores with the brutality of human behavior.

> Faultless horizon. Flattish sea.
> Wet shore. Wide plain. Look west:
>   King Menelaos sees Patroclus fall
> And thinks: "His death will get us home."

Homer's similes run a thread of relation between gods and men, heaven and earth: they reaffirm common life amid the fury of war. Dawn in Homer breaks gradually, as it does in real time. Logue renders this precisely.

Rat.
Pearl.
Onion.
Honey:
These colours came before the Sun
    Lifted above the ocean,
Bringing light
    Alike to mortals and Immortals.

Whenever I think of Tomas Tranströmer these lines
from his poem "Nocturne" come into my head:

Human beings sleep:

some can sleep peacefully, others have tense faces
as though in hard training for eternity.
They don't dare to let go even in deep sleep.
They wait like lowered gates while the mystery rolls
    past.

I often think of them while driving, or on buses and
trains and (albeit less frequently, but more intensely)
airplanes, where the faces look taut and drawn "as though
in hard training for eternity." It is in lines like these,
in which he captures the ambiance of the busy world,
that a naturally acute psychologist and a masterful poet
join forces. Tranströmer relates, is alerted to the slightest
quivering in the atmosphere, and finds solutions, imaginative
ones, while he arrives at some point of determination
through the poem. He will often tear a moment out of
time and fill it with space.

Faster and faster the water pulls

as when a river narrows down and shoots over
into rapids—I stopped to rest at a spot like that
after a drive through dry woods

one evening in June: the transistor told me the latest
on the Extra Session: Kosygin, Eban.

The tension in this poem, "Going With The Current,"
has been multiplying, finding extensions everywhere.
This crisis has been induced—he has soaked up the
anguish of others as later, in "The Couple," the lovers
will dream each other's dream in the night without
knowing it. He is also frustrated, like Thoreau, after
he has wasted an afternoon listening to his neighbors—
the human ones—cavil and babble on about what is
happening anywhere else in the world. At the same
time, Tranströmer is in another century and can't turn
his back when he sees and hears "the current/drag-
ging with it those who want to go and those/who don't."
The problems at hand are not trivial. They concern him
and they concern many people. The situation in the
Middle East, for example, imminently affects us all.
The news is like a negative infusion.

One or two thoughts bored their way in despairingly.
One or two men in the village.

And huge masses of water plough by under the
    suspension
bridge. Down comes the timber! Some trunks
just shoot straight ahead like torpedoes. Others turn
crossways, sluggish, and spin helplessly away,

and others follow their nose onto the riverbank,
steer in among stones and rubbish, get wedged,
then in a pile turn up toward the sky like folded
    hands,

prayers drowned in the roar . . .

He is riveted to the gestures of these logs running downriver, escaping from something, and not to—anything. His state of mind searches for its counterpart in the world, projects itself fully into the things themselves so that they remain entirely what they are and are transformed at the same time. The violence he perceives in nature and history, "the current," is, and is not, the violence he finds in himself since he was dragged in the wake of his friends' desperation. That is why the logs become "torpedoes." What can the imagination do, where can it find outlets when deluged with so much relevant yet unassimilable information, when even "prayers" are "drowned in the roar," become motionless in the current, and remain unheard in the furious onrush of history, whose pace has accelerated ad infinitum in the last fifty years, largely because of such things as "transistors."

The only answer out there to whatever is going on in here, inside the self, is something that might inspire stillness—to turn off even the mental chatter. Tranströmer has to find something in the landscape above the river to be an antidote to his turmoil; an involuntary sign.

> I saw heard it from a suspension bridge
> in a cloud of gnats
> together with a few boys. Their bicycles
> buried in the bushes—only the horns
> stood up.

He sees hears "it" "in a cloud of gnats." The "it" he sees is a vision of man trapped in the current of history. He has, presently, two choices: the possibility of defense, the impulse to hide. The narrator has moved in and out of the current and now stands on dry land, "a suspension bridge." Then he sees the boys. They remind him of his own boyhood, a time when he knew little or nothing of "the news," when his fear was more pristine than it is now in this negative pastoral scene, when he was allied to the animal inside him. We read "the horns stood up," and see handlebars, and what we come to see is a vision of an animal hiding silently in the depths of the thicket pricking up its horns or antlers: the terror in them is an active quivering terror. A child, pretending, might say the handlebars were an animal's horns. Tranströmer, feeling his way backward in time, regrets that he can't get in touch with the child inside him. But the image steadies him, and leads him onward. The chance object, the bicycles' horns, take on the weight of a symbol, and the body of the animal, "buried in the bushes," remains invisible and signifies, by its absence, death.

His images are often less than visible. There is a kind of big haze or aura around them. And these image clusters reverberate in silence.

* * *

What we are and where we are. The perils of contingency. The longing for something like religion without the spectre of a God. The poem as a secular prayer. His unwillingness to "tear speech out of history." How history can, for a time, become myth, in the context of the journey.

> He knew the trip had been long already,
> and the face on his watch showed years, not hours.
> ("Balakirev's Dream [1905]")

Tranströmer has found modern equivalents for myth, and ways for the most ordinary things to take on symbolic properties. His use of the car, for example, is reminiscent of Bly's in *Silence in the Snowy Fields*, yet it is less italicized, more the fact of the man on his way to work or coming home than that of the man out for a drive to cure some psychological or spiritual malaise, scanning the landscape for tropes, tropisms. He is nearly always on his way somewhere and the poem occurs when an obstacle, imagined or real and real in either case, poses some threat to motion.

In "Downpour Over the Interior," (trans. Robin Fulton) a thunderstorm turns day into night: "The lights are switched on in the middle of the summer day." This is the cue for him to let go of his social self and drift backwards into a firmer and more relaxed state of being—and not only he—"All living things huddle, closed eyes./A movement inwards, feel life stronger." At such times the shadow is not more real than the body. The body incarnates the shadow and the man becomes whole—momentarily. The self is inseparable from the landscape. He feels his nameless essential self for a while, and the poem is inseparable from the landscape evoked in the poem: self and world merge: the "I" dissolves in the "other": and there is joy and terror in the feeling provoked by the occasion, more feelings on tap than he can handle, unless the outer situation be all the more extreme.

> In the silence we hear an answer coming.
> From far away, a kind of coarse child's voice.
> It rises, a bellowing from the hill.

Tranströmer's poems are always structurally interesting. He thrusts you quickly into the action, into the arc of his imagination, the dramatic situation, and can move through narrative or image to aphorism. From experience to wisdom. The "I" in the poem is usually a social self or an ego who confronts an actor, imagines an action, that throws it into conflict with his more primitive or unconscious self and his superego/conscience=/consciousness.

The thunder and the sound welling up inside him jive. His poems can be terrifying because the threat of self-dissolution is so intense. The fragility of identity and the impinging loss of selfhood provoke the poem "out of its nest." The occasion, the chance encounter, may provoke the memory of an obscure feeling buried in his own body, or an image that brings memory to bear in its construction.

> The approaching traffic had powerful lights.
> They shone on me while I turned and turned
> the wheel in a transparent fear that moved like
>   eggwhite.
>   ("Solitude")

The insight stands in direct ratio to a given pressure. What we are taught to think of as the trimmings in any art is often the fretwork of survival. Death is the connective tissue. The confrontation with death in any aspect is one of two things— (the other being ecstasy, which I will deal with later)—that bring our full attention back to life. Clarity returns. Ambiguity dissolves.

> It felt as if you could just take it easy
> and loaf a bit
> before the smash came.
>   ("Solitude")

He trusts his imagination and comes up with images that are like mystic equations, surreptitious other dimensional perceptions. They feel like pure physical extensions of psychic space: like them or not, take them or leave them, they exist as verbal objects and the language works to carry the action of the pre-verbal imagination/to imagined scene. The language is ancillary to the situation he finds himself in, in one form or another, again and again. That's how he melds the yellow of the traffic lights and the whiteness of the snow and the mirrored glare of the ice into a "transparent fear that moved like eggwhite." The line also echoes a line from *Hamlet*, a play that takes place in another Scandinavian country, that prison, Denmark:

> (Horatio is speaking) : thrice he walkt
> By their opprest and fear-surprised eyes,
> Within his truncheon's length; whilst they, distilled
> Almost to jelly with the act of fear,
> Stand dumb, and speak not to him.
> (*Hamlet*, Act II, Scene I)

Tranströmer's image is more precise and just as irreversible. He creates tension through an uncanny sense of where the drama lies embedded in a given life situation—most often a crisis—which only the imagination can resolve—since there is no way to act it out—in the body—and survive—but his poetry itself is not uncanny. He knows himself too well for that sort of displacement—in which a man can be transformed into a cockroach *naturally*—to break through.

The tone is always that of a man who writes, as Williams says, about "what concerns him and concerns many men," and who uses whatever tools poetry—as

an art that has built-in limits in terms of how it will
unfold in time—offers him to help salvage something
essential from the rush and flux of experiences: nega-
tives that need to be held up to the light of the imagination if his life is to mean, or be, anything more than
a chain of finite actions that are erased like chalk shadows
on a blackboard.

It is Tranströmer's willingness to seek "a path thru
hell" that makes his poetry compelling. We want to
know what happens next. If this seems like a component of mystery stories it's also a primary ingredient
in literature. Tranströmer has transplanted the classic
and made it utterly contemporary. The *Elder Edda* begins:

> Young and alone on a long road,
> Once I lost my way.
> Rich I felt when I found another;
> Man rejoices in man.
>   (Translated by W.H. Auden)

"Traffic," his wildest journey into the underworld, begins:

> The semi-trailer crawls through the fog.
> It is the lengthened shadow of a dragonfly larva
> crawling over the murky lakebottom.
>
> Headlights cross among the dripping branches.
> You can't see the other driver's face.

And he will gather more momentum on this unprom-
ising journey than he has on any other; goes down in
order to rise.

And no one knows what will happen, we only know
the chain breaks and grows back together all the
    time.

* * *

They turn the light off, and its white globe glows
an instant and then dissolves, like a tablet
in a glass of darkness. Then a rising.
The hotel walls shoot up into heaven's darkness.

Their movements have grown softer, and they sleep,
but their most secret thoughts begin to meet
like two colors that meet and run together
on the wet paper in a schoolboy's painting.

It is dark and silent. The city however has come
    nearer
tonight. With its windows turned off. Houses have
    come.
They stand packed and waiting very near,
a mob of people with blank faces.
                ("The Couple")

In "The Couple" the lovers communicate osmotically. They dream each other's dream. The three quatrains could be broken down into a triad; they move from the lucid ecstasy of an intensely focused sexual feeling, to a free and delicate eroticism, to a nightmare of reproach from the blankness around them which seems all the more horrible in contrast to what they have opened up—without the intervention of the will—between themselves. If there is any guilt, it is more connected to eroticism than sex. On first glance the ending is paranoid—on second glance we recognize that they are being persecuted by something insidious because it has no affect or force: numbness. The feeling is echoed in many of Tranströmer's poems—the conflict betwen who we are and want to be for ourselves and what we must become—i.e., numb, under the blank gaze of the other.

Tranströmer uncovers the hidden aspect of the visible through what he calls "night vision." The longing for night is terribly intense in his work and stands ouside any *prix fixe* psychological categories. Tranströmer's dream life is what keeps him sane, able to stand up under pressure. He has not looked outside of himself for the inner peace he needs to go on.

> With his work, as with a glove, a man feels the
>   universe.
> At noon he rests a while, and lays the gloves aside
>   on a shelf.
> There they suddenly start growing, grow huge
> and make the whole house dark from inside.
>
> The darkened house is out in the April winds.
> "Amnesty," the grass whispers, "amnesty."
>   ("Open and Closed Space")

"Open and Closed Space" is a long short poem in which an amazing number of transformations take place. Close-up. Magnification of interior space. Long shot of house seen from outside. Time and motion study. The shadows of the clouds move and do not move, move and—stasis does not exist. And I think it is paradigmatic of Tranströmer when he is most inspired and engaged by his subject: his work envelops him. It is how he measures his universe. His landscapes are not archetypal; there are archetypes embedded in the landscapes. He has apprenticed himself to *signs*.

Politics aside, I can only emphasize how right it sounds that the grass should whisper "Amnesty . . ." which sounds like a sound the grass could make in the April winds. That is, a man, a woman—without exaggeration—could hear the grass whisper "amnesty" "out in the April winds." Onomatopeia aside, this sort of line reveals the power of poetry to reveal through the ear, and the truth unearthed, hear the plea he hears the grass whisper, indicates that there is an order beyond the arbitrary ones imposed by men on the natural world. He hears what is there to be heard, in a landscape that has soaked up its own voices.

Tranströmer gives a starkness to the material; you never know what to expect. That kind of intensity of perception comes out only "under pressure"—you're not sure what provoked it, and the more you read the more you're sure it's not traceable to its source. In "After a Death" when he writes that "the shadow seems more real than the body," he means the clear-cut silhouette of a black shadow on the snow which is then paralleled by the "black dragon scales" of the samurai's armor. The shadow on the snow is not whole anymore than the snow is whole—it is made up of particles that parallel the "black dragon scales." The magnification of details, the reduction of details, the use of long shots and close-ups is always bound to emotion and the specific emotion takes place amidst so many distractions, so much void, and such an overcrowded landscape.

> In other parts of the world
> people are born, live, and die
> in a constant human crush.
>
> To be visible all the time—to live
> in a swarm of eyes—
> surely that leaves its mark on the face.
> . . .

We all line up to ask each other for help.

Millions.

One.

("Solitude")

Tranströmer, who is by all means a moralist, avoids easy judgments. He knows that projection is evil and therefore resists the temptation to point his finger and single out the "bad guys." He takes his problems with him where he goes. This decision is crucial to the survival of his or any imagination.

> A young African found a tourist lost among the huts.
> He couldn't decide whether to make him a friend or
>   object of blackmail.
> The indecision upset him. They parted in confusion.
> ("From an African Diary [1963]")

Tranströmer reminds me of Locke, in Antonioni's film *The Passenger*, who tries to become someone else, not to lose himself so much as to be in the world in a different way, one less fraught with ambiguity. Locke is a journalist who deals in words, "abstract things" which he has come to distrust; Robinson runs guns for underdeveloped countries. Locke is willing to risk death to break through to another level of communication, to break through the known codes which reduce the meaning of different experiences. The urgency of Tranströmer's poetry is a form of controlled desperation, controlled because it wants to break through and be like "the lake" that "is a window into the earth." He is primarily a poet of images (one of the reasons that his poems come across so well in translation) which is one form of escape from ambiguity. He makes the imagination, rather than language itself, the limits of his world.

* * *

The Swedish landscape. The primacy of the elements. The brilliance of the sunlight in the cold air. The peaceful coexistence of dream and reality, the jostling of reality and dream once the unconscious is admitted to consciousness. The connection Tranströmer draws between his own dreams and the historical moment as he so often receives it via the "news." The way he posits his conflict with the demands of the social world, the demand that the self be a fortified "ego," which for him is to be categorized, and robbed, finally, of identity.

* * *

I have used Bly's translations whenever possible (there are 16 other good poems which Bly has not translated in Robin Fulton's *Selected*) except when there are bloopers like "The whole universe is full!" for "Inga tomrun någonstans här." which means what it means in Fulton's version: "No blank space anywhere here." I think Fulton conveys a subtle underside better than Bly because his rather chilly reticence is more akin, at times, to Tranströmer's tone. Bly clarifies the originals in his translations, heightens the details. Fulton has dignity and restraint where Bly has power. Just the fact that "No blank space anywhere here." is a statement of fact, rather than an exclamation, matters. And the differences in their endings for the same poem "Morning Bird Songs" (Bly), and "Morning Birds" (Fulton) is worth noting. Tranströmer has "Dikten

ar fardig." Bly renders this as "The poem is finished."
Fulton renders it as "The poem is ready." It can be
either.

Which is it then, "finished" or "ready," since the two
words are by no means commensurate in meaning—
"finished" sounds better, and it plays off the sound of
"nest," but "ready" has more connotations in English,
has within it the kernel of more possibilities than "finished," which represents the end, or final step of an
action.

> Fantastic to feel how my poem is growing
> while I myself am shrinking.
> It's getting bigger, it's taking my place,
> it's pressing against me.
> It has shoved me out of the nest.
> Dikten ar fardig.

The poem, ready to be born, and once born, abandoned, is ready to be in the world, to take a journey,
since that is the root of "fardig." ("The readiness is
all . . .") And I feel as though I had overheard an inner dialogue that began long before the poem began
and will go on long after it is "finished."

> We got ready and showed our home.
> The visitor thought: you live well.
> The slum must be inside you.
> ("The Scattered Congregation")

The reader of today is in search of hope, and he does not care for poetry that accepts the order of things as permanent. If someone is loaded with that little-known internal energy which bears the name of poetry he will not be able to escape this universal expectation, and he will search—falling, rising, again falling and searching again—for he knows that such is his duty.

(The Captive Mind)

Czeslaw Milosz is cunning in exile. It is impossible to think about his poetry without thinking about history. There is nothing he has written that does not question the historical-political foundation of our being. He brings a strange astringency to his poetry and I think that this aspect of his temperament has been tempered by California. There he can recollect horror in tranquility. And write visionary poetry—grave yet free from gravity. Vision whittled out of seafoam where seagulls cut through fog and bird cries tear the air, while the poet, weatherbound and ill, selects his age-old writing instruments, "stylus, reed, or quill," and the sun is hidden, waiting to burn through the fog.

> It is a ship in the likeness of a trireme of an Egyptian sailboat
>
> In any case the same as in the days when gods used to call from

65

island to island, their hands cupped to their mouths.

Driven by a small motor, it comes near on a Pacific
    swell.

And in the rustle of the surf, runs aground high on
    the beach.

They are running, a crowd of them. On the deck, on
    the mast,
their motley nakedness.

Until the whole ship is covered with a swarm
    opening and closing its wings,

With men and women from the end of the twentieth
    century.

Waking up I understood the meaning or, rather, I
    almost did.
                        (III: "Over Cities")

He didn't begin writing this way. His early poems
are more grounded or rooted in a particular time and
place.

And, more and more often, agape,
With my Gauloise dying out,
Over a glass of red wine,
I muse on the meaning of being this not that.

Just as quite long ago, when I was twenty.
But then there was a hope I would be everything.
Perhaps even a butterfly or a thrush, by magic.
Now I see dusty district roads

> And a town where the postmaster gets drunk every
>   day
> Out of grief at remaining identical only to himself.
>   ("What Does It Mean")

I love the way he lobs that long last line at us, as though it were commensurate with the rest of the poem rather than the keen insight and universal perception that it is. And as he moved through memory and imagination toward vision, some of the shorter poems were stranded between the void and the voice—which was on its way to becoming detached, liberated, freed from the body—and so although he calls himself a "Caliban" in comparison with Simone Weil, whom he dubs an "Ariel," his evolved poetic voice, as manifested in "From the Rising of the Sun," owes a lot to Ariel. And the element air. And Milosz flies with his own wings. As an older man he rediscovered "the living stream" that sparked, through divination and alchemy, Rimbaud in his two sustained ecstatic visionary outbursts a century ago.

"From the Rising of the Sun" resembles *The Prelude*, if we can imagine *The Prelude* being written after *The Waste Land*. In "From the Rising of the Sun" Milosz moves back and forth through his life like a shuttle, leaving out all of the transitions and connectives between experiences, real, fantasized, and otherwise. This is a long poem by present standards and yet a lot is condensed into 35 pages. Milosz stays with peak experiences, spots of time. He desires to grant language priority over external reality, to bypass what does not matter in matter, only to be brought back painfully to the reality of what was—and is. Although Milosz attempts to explain himself, to account for himself, for his position in the world and the choice he has made, the movement from stanza to stanza and from section to section is associative, alogical and atemporal, moving through impasse after impasse in six decisive movements with a syntax of recurrence as though everything had happened before: "A century in an hour." Throughout he mixes the past and present and keeps on questioning the meaning of what he remembers, of what he has lived through, witnessed, participated in.

> Who will free me
> From everything that my age will bequeath?
> From infinity plus. From infinity minus.
> From a void lifting itself up to the stars?

Nothing. And by merely asking to be released from contingencies the terror he remembers comes back: with claws. Back to Warsaw. And the other Holocaust.

> Throats
> Choking.
> Fingers sinking.
> Into Flesh.
> Which in an instant will cease to live.
> A naked heap.
> Quivering.
> Without sound.
> Behind thick glass.

> And what if that was you, that observer behind thick
> glass?
> (V: "The Accuser")

This is the fate of the witness, the survivor. He cannot choose what and when to remember the worst—it just bursts in unannounced and is loath to leave its host unscathed. That moment is—insofar as "earthly civilization" is concerned—the absolute worst for Milosz. Because force was ubiquitous. "Force" which Simone Weil, whose selected works Milosz translated into Polish, defines as "that X that turns anybody who is subjected to it into a thing." When Edgar sees his eyeless father in *Lear* he exclaims in two "asides," "O gods! Who is't can say 'I am at the worst? I am worse than e'er I was . . . And worse I may be yet. The worst is not/so long as we can say 'This is the worst.'" Milosz doesn't put it that way exactly but it is the feeling I get when passages about, around, or related to the destruction of Warsaw, which he *witnessed*, occur in his writing.

*

Other Polish poets, like Herbert and Rozewicz, write about a devastated earth but they abjure discourse and description. Much of their poetry is about the impossibility of writing directly about the holocaust in Eastern Europe. It's important, in the process of coming to terms with the differences between these poets and Milosz, to remember he was born a generation earlier, and so through all of his denials he would never relinquish eloquence, the upper register of his mind, or tone down the largeness of his native voice to the omnipresent but invisible demands of history.

Where Herbert is reductionist Milosz is expansionist. Compare Herbert's "The Stone" to Milosz's "Throughout Our Lands" and you'll see what I mean. In his capsule portrait of Herbert in his *Anthology of Postwar Polish Poetry* Milosz attests to a "deep affinity" with his work, identifies the forces that molded him and the kind of response to this experience that Milosz advocates.

> If the key to contemporary Polish poetry is the collective experience of the last decades, Herbert is perhaps the most skillful in expressing it and can be called a poet of historical irony. He achieves a sort of precarious equilibrium by endowing the patterns of civilization with meanings, in spite of all its horrors. History for him is not just a senseless repetition of crimes and illusions, and if he looks for analogies between the past and the present, it is to acquire a distance from his own times.

What Milosz says about Herbert applies to Milosz as well: each artist has his own signature which he must continually trace while agreeing on certain basic attitudes towards politics, and in refusing to separate ethics and aesthetics.

Milosz is a rigorous, if not system-prone, thinker. No one could be less laissez-faire in his attitude toward human activity. And I imagine he would feel comfortable—given the gnawing limitation of any label—being called "a poet of historical irony" given the enormous range of possibilities within that position. "Historical irony" doesn't negate directness or sincerity relative to the self in poems. It doesn't deny him reverie. It only demands that he keep an eye open at all times to the historical context of his imagined, remembered, or projected scenes. It prevents him from mistaking neurotic suffering for suffering caused by forces beyond the control of any individual. And this is another reason why his poetry is an antidote to the poetry of "the self" which aspires to tragedy but lacks sufficient context and ends up as melodrama with the "I" creating all the problems it needs to overcome.

Milosz proves that poetry doesn't need to be emotive to affect our emotions. He speaks with an austere eloquence and can, at times, turn the reader inside out, wring us dry, with language that keeps its distance. His is a decidedly impersonal voice, but combined with his transcendental stubbornness and intractability his poetry comes alive in English even though it has been translated with what seems like a deliberate flatness. Actually, it has the flatness of philosophy. Listen. "My generation was lost. Cities too. And nations./But all this a little later. *Meanwhile, in the window, a swallow/ Performs its rite of a second*" (italics mine). Now this is a pointed way of circumventing description. Even seemingly direct observations take place in mythological time. And yet . . . and yet . . . I appreciate the breathing space and the chance to imagine this swallow doing what swallows do and a more active verb or precise adjective would stop me. Instead of freezing time as Robert Lowell does in a line like "Crows maunder on the petrified fairway," Milosz unlocks it, and lets the swallow out of Nietzsche's prison house of language.

*

Auden claimed that imagery was the only thing that could always be sustained in translation. Frost, our chief disbeliever in translation, said "poetry is what cannot be translated." But Frost is talking specifically about lyrical poetry, where to lose the lilt of phrasing is, at times, to lose everything, and for the remainder to sound dead. How do you translate a phrase as subtly nuanced as "A day I had *rued*," from Frost's own "Dust of Snow"?

Reading Milosz's poems it occurred to me that something else can be retained in translation: thought. A directed point of view or attitude. Conviction. Feeling. Statement. "Child of Europe" and "Three Talks on Civili-

zation," with three sections reminiscent of Blake's "The
Marriage of Heaven and Hell," and "Auguries of Innocence," shake you up, make you stop and think.

> There can be no question of force triumphant.
> We live in an age of victorious justice.
>
> He who has power, has it by historical logic.
> Respectfully bow to that logic.
>
> . . .
>
> Grow your tree of falsehood from a small grain of
>   truth.
> Do not follow those who lie in contempt of reality.
>
> Let your lie be even more logical than the truth itself.
> So the weary travelers may find repose in the lie.
>   ("Child of Europe")

> The dark blush of anger
> the impolite reply
> the loathing of foreigners
> uphold the State.
>
> Roars at a touchdown
> slums near the harbors
> liquor for the poor
> uphold the State.
>   ("Three Talks on Civilization")

What I have called the deliberate flatness of these
poems in English brings up the whole question of how
to read poetry in translation. We can't truly estimate
the ultimate quality of poetry *as poetry* from transla-

tions, and these are particularly monotonic: we get no sense of sound: the choice has clearly been to bring across the content as such, and although this impedes our ability to evaluate his poetry it helps us get a sense of the quality of his mind, the range of his imagination, and the depth of his concerns. These come through best in the longer poems (among them the two I have just quoted, and "Throughout our Lands" in the *Selected Poems* and "From the Rising of the Sun" from *Bells in Winter*) in which he brings to the fore a large repertory of techniques: lyrical and narrative: philosophical and aphoristic.

Milosz is an incredible *writer* and I don't think the obstacles to our perceiving this are as manifest in the prose as in the poetry. In his prose the sentences and paragraphs carry weight and gather terrific momentum. His prose is phenomenally dense, lucid and multilayered. It's in a passage such as the following from *Native Realm* that we get the full flavor of his style and method of association.

> Many years after World War II, when Hitler and Mussolini were no more than specters, I found myself on the beach at the Ile d'Oléron, off the French coast north of Bordeaux. Low tide had uncovered the iron hulk of a shipwreck half sunk in the sand. The water's constant swirling had made hollows around the rusty beams, and the pools of water formed a convenient place for my son to practice his swimming. We guessed that the derelict had probably been lying there since the Anglo-American landing. It turned out to be of considerably older date. A ship flying a Uruguayan flag had run ashore there, carrying copper for the French troops who were at war with the army of

Wilhelm II. The permanence of things and the im-
permanence of people is always surprising. I touched
the bulwarks overgrown with barnacles and sea moss,
*still not quite able to accept the thought that two great
world conflicts were already as unreal as the Punic Wars*
(italics mine).

(*Native Realm*)

This is great writing: the way he proceeds from a
casual encounter to a recognition containing a general
truth is masterful. The best description I've come across
of Milosz's particular kind of complexity is this one
from Nabokov's novel *The Gift*. He calls it "multilevel
thinking," and this is the way it works:

multilevel thinking: you look at a person and you
see him as clearly as if he were fashioned of glass
and you were the glass blower, while at the same
time without in the least impinging upon that clarity you notice some trifle on the side—such as the
similarity of the telephone receiver's shadow to a huge,
slightly crushed ant, and (all this simultaneously) the
convergence is joined by a third thought—the memory
of a sunny evening at a Russian small railway station; i.e., images having no rational connection with
the conversation you are carrying on while your mind
runs around the outside of your own words and along
the inside of your interlocutor. Or: piercing pity—
for the tin box in a waste patch, for the cigarette
card from the series, *National Costumes* trampled in
the mud, for the poor, stray word repeated by the
kindhearted, weak, loving creature who has just been
scolded for nothing—for all the trash of life which
by means of a momentary alchemic distillation—the
"royal experiment"—is turned into something valuable and eternal.

This is the exact method of remembrance in *Native Realm* and the longer poems: those which have time to gather momentum.

*

Exile changes a man's order of priorities. Think of Joyce, Nabokov, and Beckett. Nabokov gave his students diagrams of the railway carriages on the Moscow-St. Petersburg line not merely to stress the specificity of detail in literature, or to give them a chance to dwell within that space as it was, but to enable himself to repossess that time more fully so that it should not vanish. The exile recreates his homeland inside his head. Often in staggering detail. He remembers things he may never have paid attention to had he remained. And Joyce and Beckett and Nabokov and Milosz would not have written what they had written had they not been exiles. It puts a man on a tightrope without a safety net. In comparison with his precursors, Milosz is a latecomer to exile, but if this had not been the case we shouldn't have the poems written before 1951 or *The Captive Mind*.

Milosz has other priorities that have more to do with folklore than "society." But he is propelled to write his poems because he senses that if he doesn't no one will remember his "city, in a valley among wooded hills/Under a fortified castle at the meeting of two rivers: . . . famous for its ornate temples" (IV: "A Short Recess").

The quest and the pressure behind many of the poems is memory. Memory as force and memory as something that must be regained, like paradise. "Of earthly civilization what shall we say?" "Tidings" is a post-apocalyptic poem written from the perspective of the cosmos. Since yesterday and all time before has condensed into a speck, or as Mandelstam says, "Light-time congeals into one beam," only memory can open it up again.

"From the Rising of the Sun" is a plumb line into memory. When Milosz casts his net, he's liable to pull up something that concerns him. "Flickering of hazy trains." A dim memory about to surface of that brief time in his life—childhood and youth—before peace became consigned to momentary outlets. He tries his brains "to gain a deity" until memory finally expands and the things that *were* tumble out as words and gather rhythm and become—through rhythm—poetry. "I attend to matters I have been charged with in the provinces." This is in part the burden of exile. He must reopen the wound, reexperience the pain and terror of his own past and by implication, that of his country and most of Eastern Europe before it was razed to rubble. Milosz keeps his distance because the pain of remembering for him is double-edged. And once he begins— "Odious rhythmic speech/Which grooms itself and, of its own accord, moves on"—there's no stopping him. This is not "creative writing," it's exorcism.

Illness, "fever," sparks the process, along with the recognition that the natural world, life and time, will only wait so long for one man's revelation: "looking at the futility of my ardent years,/I heard a storm from the Pacific beating against the window." The storm will go on long after the poet, or the poet's body, is gone. And the glass will break. It is time to come to terms, to "gird up your loins, pretend to be brave to the end/ Because of daylight and the neighing of the red horse." Milosz can only return to the child in himself, to the waters of his own origin, through the language and animism of a world which is his now only through imagination.

If Milosz cannot remember, it may mean that no one will ever know that what he lived through and loved existed for himself *and* others who are barred from remembering.

> My first awareness came with war. Peeping out from under my grandmother's cloak, I discovered horror; the bellow of cattle being driven off, the panic, the dust-laden air, the rumbling and flashing on a darkened horizon. The Germans were arriving in Lithuania and the Czarist army was retreating, accompanied by hordes of refugees.
>
> *(Native Realm)*

And it is not enough to remember. (For Basil Bunting, "It is easier to die than to remember.") Milosz must bear witness because there is no one else to do the job. And being a citizen of the world has given him the perspective with which to regain—dailiness. But first he must lose himself, set himself adrift in time, out of his body, to where he was, to be where he could never have been, to submit to the insistence of his own voice— that is another's. "Revelations of touch, again and again new beginnings, no/knowledge, no memory ever accepted" ("Whiteness").

The voice in *Bells in Winter* is often in a state of flotation. It is not, as in so many poems in *Selected Poems*, connected to its own historical moment so much as adrift and in search of it. The cosmos intervenes with history and the physical world recedes.

> Again the other, unnamed one, speaks for me.
> And he opens fading dreamlike houses

So that I write here in desolation
Beyond the land and sea.
            (I: "The Unveiling")

It is the voice of this other that resounds through "From the Rising of the Sun." Stark and impersonal. Sometimes it is hard to know the extent to which he's in agreement with the subject for whom he's speaking. "I didn't support the theses of Copernicus. I was neither for nor against Galileo's case." Because, as a man of the mind and as a poet of consummate historical imagination, Copernicus and Galileo are as real to him as the names of those he knew or valued in another country, as real to him as he predicts his own name will be to others: "An item in the fourteenth volume of the encyclopedia/next to a hundred Millers and Mickey Mouse" (V: "The Accuser"). Those two lines could stand as paradigm for poetry of voice because there is no way the body could have been present at the occasions to which he refers.

No longer in continuous time.

*

Milosz is not so much self-conscious as self-watchful. The few moments of intense lyricism in his poetry really stand out. There is this treasured moment in "Throughout Our Lands," a poem of his that I love. (The poem abounds in such moments.)

Paulina, her room behind the servants' quarters, with
    one window on the orchard
where I gather the best apples near the pigsty

squishing with my big toe the warm muck of the
     dunghill,
and the other window on the well (I love to drop the
     bucket down
and scare its inhabitants, the green frogs).
Paulina, a geranium, the chill of a dirt floor,
a hard bed with three pillows,
an iron crucifix and images of the saints,
decorated with palms and paper roses.
Paulina died long ago, but is.
And, I am somehow convinced, not just in my
     consciousness.

Above her rough Lithuanian peasant face
hovers a spindle of hummingbirds, and her flat
     calloused feet
are sprinkled by sapphire water in which dolphins
with their backs arching
frolic.

(section 11)

A non-sensual (as poets go) Caliban? Yes, because he
is proper and well mannered. *Cosmopolitan.* A Slavic
writer without a trace of *poshlust* but who has held
back an element of himself—intentionally. But these
things can never be treated as such because the will is
not the master of the self, or the free spirit. (Or is it
the master who frees the self?)

Rigorously intellectual, Milosz is not committed to
the donnée, to the chance encounter. Mandelstam was
an intellectual poet but we feel he's soaked up the poem
through the soles of his feet, his pores, that it has permeated his being and that each poem begins and ends
where it does because it has to; whereas Milosz begins
on a course and continues discursively. Where Mandelstam
is intellectual Milosz is cerebral. He writes against gravity.

Contingency. Space and time. The gyrations of the cosmos. Four-sided infinity. A mind hovering in the present tense, over a body resting in the past tense, begging to be retrieved—among the maple leaves. This body gave birth to the memory embodied in the image of a twenty-year-old "As he walks along one acrid morning . . . on the sloping little streets of a wooden town/ Since it was so long ago, in a millenium visited in dreams" (I: "The Unveiling").

The roads are not only long and crooked, they sometimes disappear for centuries. There are huge gaps of time in Milosz—gaps big enough to suggest a revision of our way of regarding earthly time as bound essentially to the natural or unnatural duration of a man's life. Milosz sees time as a double-faceted thing: there is our way of conceiving of it and the way that lies beyond our reach. It is like coming to a ditch that is too wide to cross. Milosz imagines another way of conquering obstacles rather than going forward or turning back. He obliterates the problem by changing the terms of his relation to it.

> They say somebody has invented you
> but to me this does not sound convincing
> for the humans invented themselves as well.
>
> The voice—no doubt it is a valid proof,
> as it can belong only to radiant creatures,
> weightless and winged (after all, why not?),
> girdled with the lightning.
>
> I have heard that voice many a time when asleep
> and, what is strange, I understood more or less

an order or an appeal in an unearthly tongue:

> day draws near
> another one
> do what you can
> ("On Angels")

Maybe the best way to put it is that Milosz has rejected a concept that has formed the basis of romantic poetry, "negative capability," to which poets who might not agree on anything else often cleave. From reading his essays in *The Emperor of the Earth* and elsewhere, the writers he seems to approve of most (Nicola Chiaromonte, Albert Camus and Simone Weil) are almost never poets. No matter how different he is from Brecht in form and style and attitude Milosz is allied to him in the way he sets himself strict guidelines as to what the poet's responsibility is—and he gives no quarter on this. That is why he "tends to accuse" Pasternak (in "On Pasternak Soberly") and uses the devastatingly precise phrase "programmatic helplessness" to epitomize the side on which he, and many others, erred. No act, for Milosz (or Brecht) is apolitical.

Milosz writes in the first person a poetry of statement and, with some irony, is willing to address us all, a generalized or ideal-typical other, abjuring metaphors and riddles and many other poetic devices in favor of the dithyramb—and demands of himself a lucidity so that he can't be mistaken. He wants his poetry to mean, not just "be." The problem is: how can he accomplish this and still write poetry as opposed to rhetorical tracts? The answer resides in the tone. In his ability to shift from the hieratic to the quotidian: "There is so very much death, and that is why affection for pigtails, bright-colored skirts in the wind, for paper boats no more durable than we are . . ." ("Counsels").

*

How he loves to ply contradictions. Paradoxes. And his sense of humor presses through the grimmest scenes— the trait of a survivor—amazed as he is by the fact that a question mark in back of any word or thing brings out its inherent and too often buried or con- cealed and real strangeness.

> A magpie was screeching and I said: Magpiety?
> What is magpiety? I shall never achieve
> A magpie heart, a hairy nostril over the beak, a flight
> That always renews just when coming down,
> And so I shall never comprehend magpiety.
> If however magpiety does not exist
> My nature does not exist either.
> Who would have guessed that, centuries later,
> I would invent again the dispute over universals?
> ("Magpiety")

He resolves to reach no other resolution to the con- flicts that engage him beyond the surety that there is no resolution to any of them, except an acceptance of the persistence of change.

"Magpiety" gives us a good sense of how Milosz's imagination is activated. First he hears the bird "screeching," and it is the sound that engenders his response in the human tongue, in language, and in this case the bird calls for a made-up word: "magpiety." The first half, "mag" stands for chattering, a characteristic still at- tributable to the bird as well as the man, and the sec- ond half for something human that stubborn birds like magpies mock. Magpies are as common as crows in

Europe and in America are most abundant in—where else?—California. If I dwell a little on the bird itself here it's because the poem's interest and strength are inseparable from its characteristics. I remember my own feeling of surprise when I first saw magpies perched on the loins of gargoyles in a walled medieval city in Provence. It was at once grotesque, incongruous, and true.

The magpie is ubiquitous and persistent and it is this quality that Milosz feels he "shall never achieve . . . never comprehend." His enthusiasm is self-delighting, and yet the shrug-of-the-shoulders tone with which he asks a simple question disappears entirely in lines six and seven. My response is: magpiety exists in his invention of it. It's a word, not a thing. A magpie screeches. A man cries out to himself, spontaneously, and in the process invents a word that bears enough relationship to a thing, the magpie, and other words, piety, that he is forced to think. The second half of the poem, the last four lines, and particularly lines six and seven are quintessentially Miloszian. Is he serious? Yes. Is he completely 100% straightforward serious? No. Is he being ironic again? Not exactly. Then what? That's what. What? What. Take it as far as you want. Relish the humor. Contemplate the philosophical implications. What is his "nature" anyway? I've never understood what human nature was though—I think—I understand "magpiety"— or the nature of magpies.

If his nature "does not exist either," does that mean that he doesn't exist? Are he and his "nature" inseparable? And has he really thrown everything into question to the extent that he "would invent again the dispute over universals," when it had already been solved once and for all by . . . Wait a minute. Maybe nothing was solved, maybe, just maybe, "the dispute" needs to be aired, reinvoked, again after centuries. (How many? Centuries. . . .) Here we are at the end of the poem knowing less than when we began. Now, if I could just silence those magpies. Or is it the poets, who invent words that refer to things that are and things that are not, and use these things, these words, this language, to make us worry the very foundations of our beings. I can see, following on the tail of "magpiety," another word that isn't in the dictionary, one created by human beings to define them as magpiety defines magpies. Or the magpie in man. Or . . . or the one forever wedded in my mind to the gargoyles on the columns over Les Baux.

*

The order we live in is not natural. And once nature itself is inhabited by naturalists it is no longer—in the ontological sense—natural.

> We were flying over a range of snow peaked moun-
> tains.
> And throwing dice for the soul of the condor.
> —Should we grant reprieve to the condor?
> —No, we won't grant reprieve to the condor.
> It didn't eat from the tree of Knowledge and so it
>   must perish.
>   (II: "Diary of a Naturalist")

It's hard to identify his tone—a hairs breadth between irony and anger. Detachment. A calm, even, reasoned syntax and attitude toward catastrophic events. A disciplined, versus an innate, coldness. Recognition of an impasse that must be renounced even if nothing can be done.

Before Milosz emigrated to the United States he already had an America of the mind, as evinced in the startling flashback to the classroom where he first saw the names of the birds and beasts of America written on the blackboard, giving them a kind of mythological status. This is one reason why "The Diary of a Naturalist" is riddled with doubleness. Milosz's naturalist, however pure, is as dangerous to each species of plant and animal he encounters, uncovers, and/or *names* as the pure scientist who has no control over what is done with his discoveries. This problem, which has to do with how power is used, creates a conflict that impels him to search always for analogies, most often in the form of historical precedent: to direct his energy toward humanizing a world over which the individual has less and less control and in so doing make the present time more comprehensible.

Milosz is the opposite, say, of the fiery Vallejo, (who predicted—wished?— he would die in Paris on a rainy day he could already remember) and yet Milosz's outspoken reticence can be just as wrenching at times. Tension in art has to do with the dynamics built into the work. Milosz is impassive and passionate and the result is not easy to categorize. "The voice of passion is better than the voice of reason. The passionless cannot change history" ("Child of Europe").

*

The pluperfect tense. "If only . . ." "And I would . . ." "If only I had been happy walking down Harbor Street/ (which, anyway, did not lead to a harbor/But only to wet logs beyond the sawmills.)" This memory becomes

the model for all future relations between expectations/
hope and reality/despair. In this crucial passage Milosz
locates the juncture between what's implied by a name,
which is not something he ever takes for granted, and
what it really represents. This way of making sense is
akin to Brice Parian's as interpreted by Albert Camus.

> Parian's basic idea is one of honesty: the criticism of
> language cannot get around the fact that our words
> commit us and that we should remain faithful to them.
> Naming an object inaccurately means adding to the
> unhappiness of this world. And, in fact, the vast wretch-
> edness of man.

But the poet in Milosz never loses touch with the
childlike side of himself, which is why the author of
such stern, imperious essays as "On Pasternak Soberly"
is also the visionary poet of "From the Rising of the
Sun," seeking "The living water in which all strength
revives."

The decisive line in "Bobo's Metamorphosis"—"From
childhood till old age ecstasy at sunrise"—is a good
one to return to when the body of his work turns into
a maze and you become enmeshed in a net of dialectics where thesis and antithesis are in constant flux,
and all synthesis seems to have been jettisoned. It is a
rare archetypal image connoting continuity and repetition. Not hinged to a particular place. Wherever he
has been, under whatever circumstances, this is the one
life-enhancing, rapturous feeling that remains, atemporal,
ahistorical—momentary but central, something—sometimes
the only thing he could look forward to every day of
his life—even on the morning before he says the machine guns make the cobblestones stand on end like
porcupine quills.

It is crucial that even before Poland was under siege Milosz was asking, "What can be gathered?" ("No More") and engaged in salvaging the pith of earth's offspring. His is not "public" poetry but poetry that stresses the necessary connection between art and life. Born into the *polis*, we are political beings even if we choose to leave our home country and go into exile. Joseph Brodsky hits the target in these lines from "Cape Cod Lullaby": "having sampled two oceans as well as continents, I feel I know what the globe itself knows: there's nowhere to go."

Lear speaks of "unaccommodated man" and Milosz of crushed man, of man subject to the rack, the wheel of history, tortuously bound as to "a wheel of fire," with no answer to the questions on which his sanity hinges. This unrelenting attitude, combined with his compulsion to bear witness, adds to my esteem for him. He doesn't hold back from judging his contemporaries, nor does he in any way excuse himself, or defend his expatriation beyond the fact that he didn't want to die for anything and he was lucky to have survived. In a strange way he's asking his readers to excuse him, to pardon his offenses, the main one being that he is one of the few who survived to tell the story. The other being that he is not only alive but, in his way, according to his nature, thriving, while so many others he knew were destroyed by the system they could not see through. "Chorus: He whose life was short can easily be forgiven./ He whose life was long can hardly be forgiven" ("The Unveiling," *Bells in Winter).

In a poem like "Child of Europe," Milosz's bitterness is most apparent. He transforms his anger and disgust into epigrams.

We, whose lungs fill with the sweetness of day,
Who in May admire trees flowering,
Are better than those who perished.

There's some of Lear's fool in this cruel, twisted, riddled humor. Milosz cannot forgive himself but he had no other choice than to do what he did, that is, leave, other than die.

Love no country: countries soon perish.
Love no city: cities are soon rubble.

Throw away keepsakes, or from your desk
A choking, poisonous fume will exude.

Do not love people: people soon perish,
Or they are wronged and call for your help.

Do not gaze into the pools of the past.
Their corroded surface will mirror
A face different from the one you expected.
          ("Child of Europe")

He will always disobey his own advice of this sort but his dialectical cast of mind—which in his case almost seems natural rather than learned—gives his art its edge. Milosz is rarely edgy, yet everything he has written has an edge—the moment you think you've settled on an idea, grasped his meaning, he turns it back on itself.

*

In *The Captive Mind* Milosz plays the gadfly. In 1981, some thirty years after it was published, it reads like a warning, a profound allegory of human fate; and in giving such marvelously detailed portraits of how not to live Milosz presents us with some down to earth alternatives: wariness, awareness, and cunning. The book is a polemic addressed to an audience of sleepwalkers who need more cold water splashed on their faces and less "cold war" rubbed into their eyes from the video of television screens. It can be read as though the Holocaust he refers to occurred yesterday, centuries or millennia ago and still change your life in the reading.

The captive mind is that mind which cannot—through imagery or intelligence—find solutions to exigent problems even when the solution is inherent in the very formulation of the problem. Milosz implicates himself in all of these "case studies," which is the first thing his characters, in the presence of capitulating, give up unwittingly.

*

In the last section of "From the Rising of the Sun," "Bells in Winter," he works back to his point of origin. The poignancy is echoed in the way he gently falls backward in time—and then finds his way to the truth through lying.

No, I have never been to Transylvania.

He remarks after a long passage about a mystical encounter he had "Once, when returning" from there, from "far Transylvania":

I have never brought messages from there to my
    church
But I could have.
This is an exercise in style.
The pluperfect tense
Of countries imperfective.

Had his body been able to follow the contours of his mind he "could have" been where his imagination had taken him. No such luck. No matter how truly he should choose to speak, "countries imperfective" are there to sunder the surety of connections of time and place he wants to make. Then come moments of peace before hellfire breaks loose again.

> For me, therefore, everything has a double existence.
> Both in time and when time shall be no more.

> . . .

> Bells jingle nearby, then farther away, shaggy horses
> Covered with hoarfrost, every hair distinct.
> (VI: "Bells of Winter")

Because the memory is so distant in time and because the scene is so distinctly of another time that is gone. And that Milosz in the course of his life has bridged two times: linear and cyclical. Or: circular and digital. Milosz will obliterate linear time and then return to it. Some of us don't believe that you can conquer time but in the limited context of human life this constitutes time regained.

> I could count the years. But I prefer not to.
> What are years, if I see the snow and her shoes
> Funny, pointed, buttoned on the side.
> And I am the same, though the pride of the flesh
> Has its beginning and its end.
> (IV: "Bells of Winter")

The echoes of *The Four Quartets* are pronounced and, I would guess, conscious. Even if "the fire and the rose are one" there is for Milosz no final reconciliation, no end to the interminable impasse, the crossroads at which he finds himself continually. History will always intervene and he will always be saddled with "the same consciousness unwilling to forgive."

*

In Pirandello's *Tonight We Improvise*, Ludmilla Pitoeff changed from a young girl into an old woman within a quarter of an hour. She sat on her chair in front of the footlights, and her companions, the goddesses of time, applied wrinkles to her face, erased the rouge from her lips, and scattered gray in her hair. *Never before had the horror and pity of tragedy so deeply penetrated to me. My own regular subject of contemplation was the same: the devastating process of change—in individuals, in countries, and in systems. Perhaps all poetry is simply this* (italics mine).

(*Native Realm*)

Heidegger, like Rilke's panther, is doing a kind of "orbital dance around a circle's center." This center resides in the Greek word "aletheia—the unconcealedness of beings." A philosopher who thinks that great philosophers have only one thought must be prepared to fit into his own categories. In Heidegger's case, such seeming reductionism turns out to be more fruitful than any type of pluralism because his conception of "one thought" is such that it allows for a multiplicity of interpretations, all of which are contained, but not necessarily elicited, in the thought itself. There are shapes, not a single shape, slumbering in that wood which is so important to Heidegger. It is one shape which takes many shapes. The same is true for "aletheia—which changes with every new context in which it is seen, in which it chooses to reveal itself to us."

Heidegger is spinning around a center that holds him together. "Aletheia" is a transhistorical, supratemporal truth—created, discovered, and lost in time—to be found only in time, because it, "aletheia," never changes. It is only the interpretations, the translations, the reevaluations of it that change. Godard's introduction of *La Chinoise* as "a film gone awry in the cosmos" would pertain to much contemporary French philosophy and art. Heidegger, on the other hand, has the cosmos in focus. Like Dupin in *The Purloined Letter*, he has discovered the "letter" ("aletheia") in the most obvious place, its origin in the word itself. He is trying, through reason, to release us from the bonds of rationality.

I sense that Heidegger is playing with fixed dice, because the combinations always turn up the same. He is always uncovering something, exploding any notions we might have thought were "thoughts" by showing us how they are closer to being mere "logistics," aspects of "correctness" which he detests. He is less concerned with "knowing" than with a way of knowing. Thus he incorporates the incompleteness of *Being and Time* into the motive of his project. It is not, as is usually the case, a perverse perfectionism that keeps him from finishing, but a conviction that existence is related to the process of thinking—the constant and erratic uncovering of truth on the way. When something is correct and known, it is ready to be packaged and labeled and consumed and put alongside the rest of the cans on the Shelf of Knowledge. He doesn't want his ideas to collect cobwebs by remaining static. He is insisting, as Proust does, that truth is never the result of a prior disposition towards reality but of a violence in thought. What we know beforehand we don't know. What we discover, through seeing and listening, like Rilke's Orpheus, we discover in the present.

> Animals created by silence came forward from the clear
> and relaxed forest where their lairs were,
> and it turned out the reason they were so full of silence
> was not cunning, and not terror,
>
> it was listening . . .
> And where before

there was hardly a shed where this listening could
   go,

a rough shelter put up out of brushy longings,
with an entrance gate whose poles were wobbly,
you created a temple for them inside their ears.
                    (Translated by Robert Bly)

George Trakl's poetry, more than that of anyone I
can think of, is a poetry of listening. His language is
completely in service of immediate perception. He even
gives the past the feel of presentness. The self dissolves
into the landscape and in doing so becomes the landscape. There is separation between landscape and language, word and thing: words emerge from the thickness of the world.

Heidegger likes Trakl because his words seem to come
out of an experience that is prior to language; prior,
even, to metaphor. Trakl's language is the language of
origins, of the forces that gave rise to language. He is
engaged in the primordial and magical act of naming
things. It is often said that we name things in order to
gain power over them. Heidegger, I think, would say
that we name things in order to gain contact with them
and in doing so gain contact with ourselves, our place
in the order of things.

Trakl's language inhabits the objects of its consciousness
like a spirit. They are nothing without each other. There
is only one poem, to my knowledge, in which he refers to himself as "I." It is the only poem of his where
we have any demarcation between self and world, and
what goes on between them in a series of eternally
brief and elliptical encounters.

   I am a shadow far from darkening villages.
   I drank the silence of God

Out of the stream in the trees.

Cold metal walks on my forehead.
Spiders search for my heart.
It is a light that goes out in my mouth.

At night, *I found myself* in a pasture,
Covered with rubbish and the dust of stars.
In a hazel thicket
Angels of crystal rang out once more.
                    (Translated by James Wright)

I do not doubt for an instant that the miracles are taking place. They happen to the reader at the same time they happen to Trakl. And isn't this the quintessential Heideggerian self, drinking the silence of God, finding itself (rather than consciously trying to get there) in a pasture where miracles are taking place as calmly and matter of factly as normal daily events? There is more Heidegger in the way the rather invisible, bodiless "I" regards its own dissolution and regeneration as part of the process of its being on its way, as coldly as if it were someone else, as though it was all worth it just to see and hear the crystal angels lurking in the thicket, waiting for someone to rediscover them, to bring them back to life. And much depends on the "I" being there at the right moment, because it has to be an accidental encounter.

The cold metal and the spiders bring him to the brink of death and at the same time open him up to the possibility of vision. The "angels of crystal," though invisible, are the perfect synthesis of visual and aural qualities. He sees and hears at the same moment with equal intensity. They "rang out" to let you know where you are, so you can look through them like a crystal ball that shows what is happening in the present.

What issues out of this receptiveness is speaking. Heidegger says: "Language speaks at the peal of stillness." The angels of crystal are the incarnation of this "peal of stillness," and the fact that they are ringing out "once more," connects to Heidegger's central concept of "aletheia," the unconcealing of beings that inhabit the place. History, for Heidegger and Trakl, is now in the angel waiting to be sounded.

The angel is often Trakl's double, or shadow-self. Like Rilke's angel, it is beautiful and terrible. It partakes equally of ecstasy and death. Trakl wants to integrate this shadow-self with his social or mundane self (which in his case has practically vanished anyway). The angels lead him back towards his origins, the foundations of being that linear time has buried under the rubble of history. The self, Trakl is saying, to become self, must be released from self-consciousness which implies a denial of self.

It's important that Trakl never uses similes. He presents his visions as other men might recite the soot of their day's agenda. He sees and hears what is there to be seen and heard. Comparisons, via the simile, would be worse than odious here; they would be reductive. The richness of the thing perceived in itself is superior to its potential extensions. The image is its own extension. As Blake said, "One thought contains immensity." There aren't many thoughts that do this and the "angels of crystal" may be an image, but they certainly fill the mind, situating themselves at the beginning and end of consciousness. Most poets would present this image and then go on to talk about it. Even Rilke does this. His angels are the ideas of angels. They are

intangible and immaterial. For Trakl, the acts of seeing and hearing come to life through their relatedness
without which neither of them, like world and earth,
sky and temple, would exist. I said that this image
wasn't a thought, yet it fills the mind in much the same
way as Nietzsche's thought (which Heidegger so often
quotes in *What Is Called Thinking*): "The wasteland grows."

Trakl doesn't show the wasteland growing. He gives
it to us full grown. He doesn't give us the process of
illumination but rather the illumination itself in the
state of its shining. If history, for Heidegger, doesn't
progress epoch by epoch, like brick laid upon brick,
for Trakl, all of history happens at once; has in essence, already happened. The poet is not innovative.
He discovers what is already there. Countless incidents
have merged into a few images. Trakl doesn't see the
modern world in terms of the ancient, because that would
imply something like a linear development, something
like progress.

In his discussions of science and mathematics,
Heidegger criticizes these disciplines for being cut
off from their foundations, their underlying mo-
tives, questions of ontology like (to quote Scheler),
"Progress? Progress towards what?"

Trakl doesn't dress up his myths in modern costumes.
(Such a practice is usually parodistic, and Trakl proves
that Marx's dictum about tragedy turning into farce
the second time around is not uncontestable.) His myth
is present in the act of his *being there*, of his invisible
self infusing with the landscape with life. He is always leaping onto the ground on which he already
stands. He, or the beings that populate his poems, are
always underway, always on their way.

Wanderer in black wind; lightly the dry reed
Whispers in the stillness of the moor.
    ("On the Moors," translated by Robert Grenier)

His most frequent persona is that of a wanderer. Trakl's wanderers, Heidegger's "being" that is "on its way," have apprenticed themselves to signs. They are trying to decipher the hieroglyphics that they encounter. They are attentive to sounds and places, rather than "time and space."

The wanderer brings "being" into an encounter with danger. He is always in danger of getting lost, of losing his way. He is only prepared to lift his leaden eyelids at nightfall, when the sun "breaks from gloomy ravines." He walks "in the black wind" to be able to hear the "dry reeds rustling quietly through the silence of marshy pastures." The obstruction of normal vision forces his senses to wake up. His seeing eye is anything but like a camera. His pulses quicken. He must perceive everything in order to survive the journey. That is why, for Trakl, everything rests on the perception of the slightest quivering in the atmosphere. Wandering is the bridge between life and death. Illumination stands on one side, death on the other.

Heidegger chooses to talk about "A Winter Evening" because it is more in accordance with his thoughts about gathering, collecting, usefulness, reliability, and dwelling, than Trakl's other wanderer poems, one of which—"Towards Nightfall My Heart"—I can't resist quoting for its terrible delirious joyfulness.

At nightfall one hears the crying of bats,
Two black horses frisk in the meadow,

The red maple rustles.
To the wanderer the little wayside inn appears.
Glorious new wine and walnuts taste to him,
Glorious: to stagger drunk through the dusking
    wood.
In its black branches the grievous bells are pealing.
Dew-drops fall on his face.
              (Translated by M. Hamburger)

The wanderer performs the leap into the present, into the taste of things. And this is where Heidegger is leading us, towards the sensuousness of a time and space that pulsate. Heidegger risks the abyss. He jumps right in front of us, and when he does not fall downwards, when he lands on the ground on which he already stands, we see it's possible to "fall upwards to a height," to walk into time, reeling, on a tightrope that is suspended between two points of air—a taut wire of nothing surrounded by nothing but an invisible echo that represents the accumulated noise of history.

At night the autumn woods cry out
With deadly weapons and the golden plains,
. . . the night embraces
Dying warriors, the wild lament
Of their broken mouths.
       ("Grodek," translated by M. Hamburger)

The echo extends from the shadows, where the ghosts of heroes, "the bleeding heads," appear now as they have always appeared. The *historical* past is imbedded in the landscape. We never doubt the reality, even the factuality of his visions. They reek of war more than any objective journalistic report. And yet it is not an abstract archetypal battle, but one that is imbued, through

Trakl's immersion in a present war, with the viscosity
of the night, who, like a woman (though the night is
not strictly and boringly personified), like something
more feminine than female, "embraces the dying warriors." The woods are given their existence by the beings that inhabit them and by the earth from which
they spring up. Trakl isn't just giving the woods human qualities. The cry of the woods is the cry of the
world that has soaked up its own voices. History happens seldom, but nothing is forgotten. Battles have taken
place in these woods before.

But it is not the soldiers who bring the woods to
life. The woods are crying out with wind as well as
assault. Trakl listens. The woods hear him listening
and they cry out in response to his silence. There are
precedents . . .

> Roland has set his ivory horn to his mouth: he puts his
> lips hard against it and blows with all his strength . . .
> blows a blast on his ivory horn, and the bright blood
> flows from his mouth, and the veins burst on his fore-
> head, but the sound of the horn swells and mounts, and
> Charles hears it . . . Duke Naimes hears it: "That horn is
> the sound of Roland's despair!"
>   (Translated by W.S. Merwin)

Roland's song only exists insofar as Charles and the
Duke of Naimes are there to respond to it. They listen
to its appeal and identify it with a particular emotion:
despair. The passing on of his desperate message is
what makes Roland, in Heidegger's phrase, "capable
of death as death." Roland is an actor. Trakl's wanderer is bound to pure perception, without the inter-
mediary of an Ego. His actions come into being through
the perception of the poet. These, in Heidegger's terms,

"visible inclusions of the alien in the sight of the familiar" are what make the alien alien and the familiar familiar. Just as the striving between world and earth imparts identity to both, so poetry helps man "take measure of his dwelling."

The pain of the warriors, both in Trakl and *The Song of Roland*, is transpersonal. It is the pain of all warriors who ever existed. The landscape in Grodek has soaked up its history. The deadly weapons seem to have been there a long time, perhaps as long as the forest can remember. So history becomes a series of invisible accretions waiting to be illuminated, waiting to be heard. But it is not the poet, George Trakl, pharmacist first class, who hears what is there. What is there is there to be heard. That is why it is there. There is no time for personality in Trakl, and this is in accord with Heidegger's thought about great art being supremely impersonal. Transcendence, if such as thing exists, is accomplished in the act of recognition, the lightning flash of perception.

Trakl's imagination digs effortlessly, even involuntarily, beneath the "lie of culture" to get to a well of darkness and silence that seems to be composed of pure energy, the bones and roots of being. Heidegger wants to get under the skin of history. He even wants to get under the bone to find out what makes bone bone.

In "Grodek," the god, ghost, or spirit of the forest emerges. Insofar as the word conveys the forest, the forest is spoken by language. All language is not speaking. The language of the forest is speaking because it comes out of the forest. It had to listen before it could speak. The closer language comes to being another aspect or extension of technology the less it speaks. Within the poem itself, the forest is like the Greek temple which "makes visible the invisible space of air." Language is used as a sign. Heidegger is not interested in the language which reveals by not revealing, the language of absences. For Heidegger, language can be about language because it originates in a prior lived experience whose essence is in language. The word is a thing that comes out of something that isn't a word. "Aletheia" is a word that denotes something. The wanderer reveals the road to itself, but it is a real road out there.

Robbe-Grillet has written that "Kafka's staircases lead somewhere." Heidegger's belief in the potency of the word makes him allergic to word games, "experiments with language." He wants something closer to what Gary Snyder calls "A riprap upon the slick rock of metaphysics."

For Heidegger, the more the artist's personality invades his work, the less the artist has given himself over to the inner life of things around him which need to be unconcealed. The work gets its workly quality from being thought about. The meaning of revelation is in revelation. "To reflect on language means," Heidegger writes, "to reach the speaking of language in such a way that this speaking takes place as that which grants an abode for the being of mortals."

A WINTER EVENING

When the snow falls on the window
The vesper bells chime a long time.
The table is set for many,
The house is well provided.

Several wanderers
Come to the door on dark roads.

Golden blooms the tree of graces
From the earth's cool liquor.

The wanderer steps in quietly;
Pain has turned the threshold to stone.
There, in the brilliant light,
On the table are bread and wine.
(Translated by Mark Rudman)

The fourfold—the primary oneness of earth and sky, divinities and mortals—are all represented in this poem. The window on which the snow falls is in this instance the bridge that "gathers to itself in its own way, earth and sky, divinities and mortals."

The wanderer invests the scene with being. The essence of wandering, being on your way, is contrasted with the non-being of those who live in the house. But there is a doubleness to his gift. The threshold turns to stone because he reminds it of what it has been missing in its service as a mere object—something to be stepped on, vehicle for passage.

No one who lives in the house notices anything about it. It is the wanderer who comes to remind them that they must "ever learn to dwell." The wanderer, the man who by definition is without a home, a dwelling, gives the dwelling back to itself in an act of presencing, of stepping in, remaining on his way while stopping to rest.

Like the snow that falls on the window, wanderers don't stay around too long. But his homelessness gives him access to the miraculous, thus his presence in "A Winter Evening" makes the bread and wine luminous, even sacred. He gives it back the aura which has been numbed by dailiness.

light or even candlelight. It is the same light that has guided him along the dark road, uncovering the path ahead of him. He draws his light from the darkness without which nothing could be "unconcealed." The wanderer, being on his way, perpetually dies with each arrival and is reborn with each departure.

For Heidegger, the poet's light is his language. "Mortal speech is a calling that names, a bidding which, out of the simple onefold of the difference, bids thing and world to come." And so when Pablo Neruda writes: "there is death in the bones/like a pure sound/like a barking without a dog/. . . Death comes to the sonorous/like a shoe without a foot/like a suit without a man," he reveals death in its embodiment in absences. These similes, incidentally, are as effective as Trakl's pure statements precisely because they point to something that is not there. He brings both death and its shells alive for us, just as water in motion gives a fountain its stillness.

For Heidegger, the word is flesh. "Aletheia" determines the presence of everything present, but there is less and less present all the time. Our origins are covered up by the rubble of history. Nevertheless, this word "aletheia" has for Heidegger the solidity of a thing. It exists whether or not we ever consciously refer to it. It is beyond us, beneath us, above us, inside us. Everything that is present is founded on it yet it remains invisible.

What we see of history, which is by default all there is to see of it, is contained in "aletheia." So far we've seen only an endless petticoat, and from this we've reconstructed the body of a sphinx. But the scent we lay down does not lead us back to our tracks.

"Aletheia" is nothing in itself and yet it doesn't ex-

"Aletheia" is nothing in itself and yet it doesn't exist as an abstraction. It reveals itself only in "minute particulars." Everything that happens to be true is so out of a happy accident in which something, anything, gets "unconcealed" revealed to itself and to us. According to Heidegger, the Greeks rejected "aletheia" in the name of a kind of linear development of thought, and history since that time has constructed a veritable Babel on a foundation it cannot see and has no inkling of.

Heidegger's anguish is related to the absurdity and futility and built in self-defeat of this project. He may write as though recent history had never occurred, but it permeates his philosophy to such an extent that the totality of his work seems to have grown out of his own time. He is engaged in the process of reconstruction. One of his and our problems is this: we may have only the facsimiles or imitations of the original materials. By this time it's nearly impossible to tell which are the natural faults in the rock and which have been blasted in. In other words, the problem is to tell the original from the derivative. Heidegger, at least, is convinced that the concept of "aletheia" is an original which by its nature can't be tampered with by time. In Trakl, Heidegger sees someone who is constantly bringing truth to light. Words and things are locked in an embrace, and you can't tell one from the other. He reinstates the primordial art of naming. In order to do so he must feel that there is something sacred left to name, or at least that the act of naming itself is sacred.

Culture is gloss, a distinction. But this line or thought really culminates in Rilke. Rilke, who consciously tried to watch and listen, would sit for hours looking at the panther in the zoo, trying to catch the core of its being in its physical inflections, gestures, signs.

THE PANTHER

His gaze, wearied by the bars going by,
retains nothing more, as if
a thousand bars were there
with nothing standing behind them.

The gentle gait of supply muscled steps
is like an orbital dance
around a circle's center
where a vast will torpidly stands.

But when from time to time the retinal curtain
splits apart, an image goes in, rushes
through the tense stillness of the limbs—
and explodes in the heart.
                 (Translated by Mark Rudman)

His poems have a primitive sophistication, as do many
of the best modern poems, which don't speak through
a persona but rather become the object of their intentions, the Creature.

Trakl neglects to displace the human world into the
creature world simply because his poems affirm that
this *is* the creature world, and we need only look at
ourselves, at our hands like hands, to leap onto the
ground on which we already stand, to be the forces
we imagine creatures to possess.

                                        1973

The Mystery of the Charity of Charles Péguy, by Geoffrey Hill.

Geoffrey Hill's *The Mystery of the Charity of Charles Péguy* is a book-length poem which takes its inspiration from Péguy's own *The Mystery of the Charity of Joan of Arc.* Hill intends no ambiguity as regards his attitude toward his subject: "Péguy, stubborn rancours and mishaps and all, is one of the great souls, one of the great prophetic intelligences, of our century. I offer *The Mystery of the Charity of Charles Péguy* as my homage to the triumph of his 'defeat.'" The poem opens with the "crack of a starting pistol," and Jean Jaurès, once Péguy's ally in his support of Alfred Dreyfus, now his enemy through his manipulation of those ends, lies dead. Hill ponders: did Péguy kill Juarès? Did he incite the assassin? But the real issues at stake here are belief and the power of the word.

We should be able to respond to a poem without researching the subject, and it is possible to read Hill's poem without knowing anything in advance about Péguy. It helps to know that he owned a bookstore and edited the journal *Cahiers.*

> This is no old Beauce manoir that you keep
> but the rue de la Sorbonne, the cramped shop,
> its unsold *Cahiers* built like barricades,
> its fierce disciples, disciplines and fueds

that he was a socialist and a poet whose work was

"confined to a small intellectual elite" in his own time; that he became a symbol of liberty, of human possibility, freedom and integrity in France; that he died when he stood up to chase the German Army in retreat; and that he had written about death on the battlefield before he died. "Dying, your whole life/fell into place," Hill writes.

> Péguy said
> "why do I write of war? Simply because
> I have not been there. In time I shall cease
> to invoke it." We still dutifully read
>
> "heureux ceux qui sont morts."

There used to be the sense that poetry issued from another consciousness, somewhere deep in the mind—"far back," as Roethke put it. Hill's poetry is of this order: bracing and difficult, turbulent and complex. There is pressure on every word to *mean*, and in this poem, the language bears the same stress as Péguy's life, as if, imbued with the desire to mate, each word were propelling itself toward the next:

> bees thrum
> in the crimped hedges and the pigeons flirt
> and paddle, and sunlight pierces the heart-
>
> shaped shutter-patterns in the afternoon

With the same momentum, Péguy imagined victory for Dreyfus, and for France over Germany ("Rather the Marne than the *Cahiers*"), and hurled himself into action.

Péguy thought of writing as taking dictation; he scorned revision, as it interfered with a divine process. His highest praise for a given piece of writing was: "It is dictated." Catholic and socialist, he praised the dignity of labor with a fervor both religious and political. In his life he combined meditation and action. Hill characterizes Péguy's epiphany in these inspired lines:

> Hedgers and ditchers, quarrymen, thick-shod
> curés de campagne, each with his load,
> shake off those cares and burdens; they become,
> in a bleak visionary instant, seraphim
>
> looking toward Chartres, the spired sheaves,
> stone-thronged annunciations, winged ogives
> uplifted and uplifting from the winter-gleaned
> furrows of that criss-cross-trodden ground.

The "people" are transformed as they sacrifice themselves for Péguy's sacred "terre charnelle," carnal earth.

Hill's art is vastly more demanding than Péguy's; his courage and daring are aesthetic and linguistic. But both poets reach out toward something central to the human condition. Hill relies heavily on the traditional language of English poetry, from Shakespeare to Auden: "The world is different, belongs to them—/the lords of limit and contumely." From the key placement of the word "contumely" and the phrase "the lords of limit" and his use of the latter as the title of his new book of essays *The Lords of Limit*, Hill seems to be saying that things have not changed as much as we may think. His words have a gravity that is more powerful than sound effects or particular images. In "Redeeming the Time," he refers to "the inertial drag of speech," which must be accounted for by any "enquiry into the nature of rhythm."

Without being visual, his poetry makes you imagine a backdrop of the Renaissance—paintings and tapestries with battle scenes—a thicket of world in a thickness of words, as in this hard-earned and revealing passage from an earlier volume of prose poems *Mercian Hymns*:

> He willed the instruments of violence to break
> upon meditation. Iron buckles gagged; flesh
> leaked rennet over them; the men stooped,
> disentangled the body.

> He wiped his lips and hands. He strolled back to
> the car, with discreet souvenirs for consolation
> and philosophy. He set in motion the
> furtherance of his journey. To watch the Tiber
> foaming out much blood.

Children scavenging in the ruins. "Swathed bodies in the long ditch; one eye upstaring." Omnipresent mud. There is no relief from this blood and the obsession with violent death.

Hill's early work is sharp and direct. It consists mainly of short poems, each one a whole: "true sequences of pain." His affinities are clear through his fine homages to Celan in *Tenebrae* and Mandelstam in *King Log*. And there is no mistaking the ferocity in his work. Ted Hughes's *Crow*, to make the inevitable comparison, is playful set beside Hill's darkest passages.

In "Funeral Music," an essay at the end of *Mercian Hymns*, he tells of "attempting a florid grim music broken by grunts and shrieks" and, in an image that is emblematic of his own project, cites "the chronicler of

Croyland Abbey" as "writing that the blood of the slain
lay caked with the snow which covered the ground
and that, when the snow melted, the blood flowed along
the furrows and ditches for a distance of two or three
miles." And, one might add, from there into the body
of his next decade's work.

In *The Mystery of the Charity of Charles Péguy*, Hill's
violence has found release through the use of the third
person. He interweaves his own voice with Péguy's;
he filters his concerns through Péguy and, in the process, gains a levity absent from his earlier work, though
the tone is one of "dour panache" (to borrow a phrase
from the poem), a cross between low tragedy and high
farce:

> A rooster wails remotely over the marsh
> like Mr. Punch mimicking a lost child.
>
> At Villeroy the copybook lines of men
> rise up and are erased. Péguy's cropped skull
> dribbles its ichor, its poor thimbleful,
> a simple lesion of the complex brain.

Hill has always been at home with the sublime. He
applauds Péguy's willingness to sacrifice, as long as a
moral code is constant, in a style that is dense, not
ornate. But he also sees human suffering as a consequence of history's mischeviousness—except that the
joke is at our expense. "History commands the stage
wielding a toy gun,/rehearsing another scene"; it is
perverse, at once "supreme clown" and "dire trage-
dian." Péguy allows him to introduce an element missing
from his previous books: humor, albeit a kind of black
humor, closer in essence to Webster and Ford than to

Heller or Pynchon. Listen to this passage, timed to the rhythm of the newsreel:

> The brisk celluloid clatters through the gate;
> the cortège of the century dances in the street;
> and over and over the jolly cartoon
> armies of France go reeling towards Verdun.

Hill is precise, careful to show how tenuously meaning cleaves to a comma, a line break: "To dispense, with justice; or, to dispense/with justice." His harsh, crabbed style, with its rugged diction, does not lend itself to length. The quatrain is his primary medium in all his books, and he has few, if any, contemporary rivals in his ability to handle it:

> This fear strikes hard and is gone
> And is recognized when found
> Not only between dark and dawn,
> The summit and the ground.
>   ("Metamorphoses," *For the Unfallen*)

And from *Tenebrae*, the book that precedes *The Mystery of the Charity of Charles Péguy*:

> I shall go down
> to the lovers' well
> and wash this wound
> that will not heal

His variable rhyme schemes, alternating *a a b b* and *a b b a*, with the more conventional *a b a b*, argue against monotony. And he writes as though the solution were locked in the quatrain itself. Péguy also used the quatrain frequently, but his formal impulse was almost

the opposite of Hill's: where Péguy expands, Hill con-
tracts. The only time the sections in *The Mystery of the
Charity of Charles Péguy* run on is in the poem's most
significant stanza, when Péguy meets the death he has
so assiduously sought, his own:

> So, you have risen
> above all that and fallen flat on your face
>
> 5
>
> among the beetroots, where we are constrained
> to leave you sleeping and to step aside
> from the fleshed bayonets . . .

It is through such density that a poem of only 400 lines
can make a book.

There are some false moves in the poem tonally, a
certain archness, as when he refers to Rimbaud's "Je
est un autre" as "that fatal telegram," and reminds me
that I prefer him where he's more cryptic and elliptical. Hill's strange brand of academic formality (which
mars the essays in *The Lords of Limit*) is also off-put-
ting in his otherwise concise and informative afterword.
Citing T. S. Eliot's interest in Péguy—clearly to establish Péguy's undeniable importance to his audience—
he writes that "T. Stearns Eliot, M.A. (Harvard), who
made reference to Péguy's life and work in a series of
university extension lectures in 1916, noted that he 'il-
lustrates nationalism and neo-Catholicism as well as
socialism.'" It is hard to tell whether he is trying to
parody the academic or embody it.

Hill is one of the few contemporary poets whose work
must be reread in order to be understood. He forces

the reader to sound out the meaning: work of this density can only be grasped through the ear. He is not merely one of the best English poets but one of the best poets writing in English. Although I think *Mercian Hymns* is Hill's best work, *The Mystery of the Charity of Charles Péguy*, shows him stretching in new directions, rescuing himself from direness, becoming more attuned to dramatic possibilities, and enlarging his range.

The Selected Poetry of Yehuda Amichai, edited and translated by Chana Bloch and Stephen Mitchell.

Yehuda Amichai is one of the half-dozen leading poets in the world. He has found a voice that many have sought and has found a way to speak across borderlines and cultures. Amichai was born and lived in Germany until he was twelve, and if he had not moved to Palestine (now Israel), he might have written in German or English, rather than Hebrew. He looks at life with a kind of triple-sightedness, with the outsider's eye for the luminous detail. He makes conflicts of the citizen soldier in modern, embattled Israel stand for those of modern man. What happens to the self in his poems reverberates through the body politic. His tone is so sure he can say anything and employs hyperbole to give an added sting to his words and defuse sentimentality.

> if I pull out the stopper
> after pampering myself in the bath,
> I'm afraid that all of Jerusalem, and with it the whole
>   world,
> will drain out into the huge darkness.
>   ("You Mustn't Show Weakness")

Amichai's work is governed by a single trope: the body is the world body—alive, sensual, fleshy and in it the private and the public come together for better:

When you do nice things to me
all the heavy industries shut down.
("Poems for a Woman")

and for worse:

They amputated
your thighs from my hips.
As far as I'm concerned, they're always
doctors. All of them.
("A Pity. We Were Such a Good Invention")

Assia Gutmann, in her earlier translation, called them "surgeons," ("They are all surgeons. All of them.") and the sense and syntax of her lines retain a striking accusatory music of their own.

Translation is a matter of coincidence. The translator doesn't seek the right word so much as the spirit of the phrase. If he is lucky he will find a style that corresponds to that of the original text. In the case of Marquez, for instance, the immediate resource is Faulkner; in the case of Neruda and Vallejo, it is Whitman. In Yehuda Amichai's case, it is the Bible, notably the Psalms and the Song of Songs. It is no accident that the psalmic and prophetic strains of his poetry translate as well as they do.

Another reason Amichai's poetry translates well is his imagery, the one thing that can with any certainty be translated in poetry. "Children move with the footsteps of someone else's grief/as if picking their way through broken glass" ("Seven Laments for the War Dead"). Drawn from myth and history and common experience, his imagery unlocks a world that is not the property or domain of one language. ("In a language that once described/miracles and God, to say car, bomb, God" ["National Thoughts"].)

This transformation of the self and its language has been accomplished before but, except in the case of Blake, mainly in epics: Joyce, Williams in *Paterson*, Olson in *The Maximus Poems*. This method of metaphor in which the body becomes the world body allows Amichai to be quick, lyrical, and cryptic and still make larger outward connections. In fact, he cannot avoid it, and envisions his "life/turned into a revolving door." A private man forced to wear a public mask, he sings of division. Yet the strain he feels in his life does not come across as strain in his work.

> All the days of his life my father tried to make a man
>   of me,
> so that I'd have a hard face like Kosygin and
>   Brezhnev,
> like generals and admirals and stockbrokers and
>   financiers,
> all the unreal fathers I've established
> instead of my father . . .
>
>   . . .
>
> I have to screw onto my face the expression of a hero
> like a lightbulb screwed into the grooves of its hard
>   socket,
> to screw in and to shine.
>   ("Travels of the Last Benjamin of Tudela")

Tried to *make* a man of me, a "man" who exists in the public sphere, and who will speak for others. As we can see from this wry self-portrait, Amichai knows how to leaven hard truths with humor.

But Amichai only embraces the public sphere through the self. In an early poem he compares his life to Venice:

everything that is streets in others is "love, dark and flowing" within him. He submits all of his experience to the pressure and presence of love before they can make their way into a poem. In this way he has, and no mere feat this, reclaimed the genre of the love poem for serious poetry. Personal without being private, serious without being solemn, he seeks relief and ease through the balm of love, writes as a man motivated to "go out to all of [his] wars" and comes back on account of love.

Amichai adopts a prophetic tone with remarkable ease. "He doesn't have seasons enough to have/a season for every purpose" ("A Man Doesn't Have Time"). When we speak—wrongly—of Biblical simplicity we mean the manner of address, a certain directness, not an inherited "wisdom." From the beginning Amichai was able to say what he was thinking rather than find a metaphor for it. Metaphors are contained within the body of his poems rather than as a casement for the poem. (I know a good poet who, bowled over by Amichai's unforced directness, stopped writing for a year when he first read his work.) For Amichai's poems begin where most poems end. He begins without a mask, with the screen torn off and the scream in its place.

> Now that I've come back, I'm screaming again.
> And at night, stars rise like the bubbles of the
>   drowned,
> and every morning I scream the scream of a newborn
>   baby
> at the tumult of houses and at all this huge light.
>   ("Jerusalem, 1967")

Amichai has been blessed in his translators: Assia Gutmann, Ted Hughes, Harold Schimmel, and now Chana

Bloch and Stephen Mitchell. They have all ably conveyed the concrete particulars of his world, but Bloch
and Mitchell get inside the text and render a subtler,
more complex, and formally expert Amichai than we
have seen before in English.

Friends who know both languages think that the Mitchell/
Bloch translation is not only excellent but that it has
superceded the earlier translations. Those of us who
have been reading Amichai since the first translations
appeared find it difficult to shake free of their authority. Ted Hughes is the presiding force over Amichai's
first two volumes in English. I would conjecture that,
as Assia Gutmann's husband, he had a definite influence on the texture of the language in *Poems*, Amichai's
first volume in English; and he translated, in collaboration with Amichai, the second book *Amen*. I even
detect a Plath/Hughes voice in many of the lines.

There's a world of difference in the placement of a
word. Assia Gutmann translated a line in one of his
most memorable lyrics as "Hair dark above his thoughts,"
which isolates in an uncanny way the hair from the
head, locates the source of the thoughts in the brain
beneath the hair, turns the physical perception into an
image of the character's psychological and spiritual condition
and, in doing so, interprets the "thoughts" for us.

> Out of three or four in a room
> One is always standing at the window.
> *Hair dark* above his thoughts.
>   ("Out of Three or Four in a Room")

Stephen Mitchell's version returns us to the thing itself, *"his dark hair* above his thoughts." Her image stresses
displacement, isolation; his line—and he also uses a
comma after the preceding line instead of a period—

stresses continuity of being in the world, ordinariness.

Criticism tends to locate difficulty in poetry on the surface of language. Because a poet says what he means does not automatically mean it is an easy matter to understand him, and Amichai narrates events that take on meaning as the "story" unfolds in time. On reading the *Selected Poems*, it occurred to me that Amichai's poetry resembled that of James Wright more than any other contemporary American poet. Both poets are able to submerge their imaginations in momentary events; both root their poems in specific places (Israel, The Midwest) and move from the anecdotal to the eternal; both use a narrative voice but write lyrics rather than narrative poems; both explore the possibilities of poetry through contexts as much as language itself. They share the capacity to speak directly but retain an eerie edge to what they say—and unsay:

> The carp are secrets
> Of the creation: I do not
> Know if they are lonely.
> The poachers drift with an almost frightening
> Care under the bridge.
> ("Lifting Illegal Nets By Flashlight")

> America,
> Plunged into the dark furrows
> Of the sea again.
> ("Stages on a Journey Westward")

> *

> Jerusalem, the only city in the world
> where the right to vote is granted even to the dead.
> ("Jerusalem, 1967")

Dicky was hit.
Like the water tower at Yad Mordekhai.
Hit. A hole in the belly. Everything
came flooding out.
    ("Seven Laments for the War-Dead")

Amichai, longing to be released from the burden of memory at the end of a long incantation, pleads: "Let *all of them* (the scrolls, the flags, the beasts, the birds) remember so I can rest" (my emphasis, "Jerusalem, 1967"). It is our good fortune that he is not likely to be granted his wish.

Report From The Beseiged City, by Zbigniew Herbert, translated by John Carpenter and Bogdana Carpenter.

I first read Zbigniew Herbert in Czeslaw Milosz's anthology *Post-War Polish Poetry*, a book that has influenced a generation of American poets. At the time, I was struck by his purity of diction and the strange blend of irony and negation in such poems as "Elegy of Fortinbras," "Study of Objects," and "The Stone." Milosz's description of Herbert as "a poet of historical irony" is apt because his work is critical in spirit:

> a murderous power is held by the zeitgeist
> that is the devil of fashion the devil of passing time
> the epoch's clock stops—the gods go down to the
> bottom
> ("Isadora Duncan")

> our further coexistence will probably follow
> a geometrical law—two parallel lines
> unearthly patience and inhuman faithfulness
> ("In Memoriam Nagy László")

"The Stone" exemplifies a poetry that attempts to salvage the remains of civilization. It is a poem that has become as integral to our way of looking at things as Wallace Stevens's "The Snow Man":

> The stone
> is a perfect creature

equal to itself
mindful of its limits

filled exactly
with a pebbly meaning

with a scent which does not remind one of anything
does not frighten anything away does not arouse
  desire

its ardour and coldness
are just and full of dignity

I feel a heavy remorse
when I hold it in my hand
and its noble body
is permeated by false warmth

—Pebbles cannot be tamed
to the end they will look at us
with a calm and very clear eye
                    ("The Stone")

What does this poem tell me about the state of things
when it praises an object for having "a scent which
does not remind one of anything," save that memory
has only one route: to pain? "The Stone" could be mistaken
for a minimalist gesture; but it isn't minimalist, it's
metaphysical. The sparest poetry may ultimately be the
richest. As Herbert says in "Mr. Cogito and the Imagination":

there is no place in it
for the artificial fires of poetry

he would like to remain faithful
to uncertain clarity

It is a miracle in our overblown world to find something that is equal to itself. A stone is not subject to much self-inflation. Herbert practices a humanistic dehumanization of art. Reality stands independent of his/our designs upon it.

Obsessed with precision, he has written a bizarre homage to that quality in "Mr. Cogito on the Need for Precision":

> because even what
> is happening under our eyes
> evades numbers
> loses the human dimension
>
> somewhere there must be an error
> a fatal defect in our tools
> or a sin of memory
>
>   . . .
>
> ignorance about those who have disappeared
> undermines the reality of the world
>
> it thrusts into the hell of appearances
> the devilish net of dialectics
> proclaiming there is no difference
> between the substance and the specter

Herbert's work has close philosophical links with that of Eastern European poets such as Paul Celan, Vasko Popa and Janos Pilinsky. These poets reduce their field of inquiry while at the same time enlarging their possibilities of vision. And so their minds turn to fable and other rigorous ways of saying that have moral rather than aesthetic priorities. Take the title poem of the book, "Report from the Besieged City." Even if the "besieged city" is actually Warsaw, Herbert raises it to an archetype, as if that unremitting state of siege were an extreme and accurate image of the human condition:

> I write as I can in the rhythm of interminable weeks
>
> . . .
>
> I avoid any commentary I keep a tight hold on my
>   emotions I write about the facts
> only they it seems are appreciated in foreign markets
>
> . . .
>
> the siege has lasted a long time the enemies must
>   take turns
> nothing unites them except the desire for our
>   extermination
> Goths the Tartars Swedes troops of the Emperor
>   regiments of the Transfiguration
> who can count them
> the colors of their banners change like the forest on
>   the horizon
> from delicate bird's yellow in spring through green
>   through red to winter's black

Herbert puts the quasi-dramatic monologue to brilliant use. The irony is in the floating "I," half a historical personage and half Herbert, a time-traveler, who is and is not the poet, who is and is not Claudius, Fortinbras, Damastes/Procrustes or various nameless narrators. I imagine him writing as if fearful that someone is looking over his shoulder—much of his meaning is insinuated and much is left to innuendo. The result is a kind of code, as though someone had launched into a complicated and emphatic explanation of how the

SHORTSTOP covers SECOND and THIRD base, but
that it is difficult for him to throw out the runner on
his way to FIRST if he has to backhand a ground ball
while MOVING to his RIGHT. A listener who already
knew the facts of the matter could interpret the emphatic capitals to mean: We can never rest because nothing
ever comes to us directly.

American poetry remains a highly private affair, but
Eastern European poets feel they have permission to
speak for humanity, and without a trace of self-con-
gratulation, as in Herbert's "The Power of Taste":

> It did not require great character at all
> we had a shred of necessary courage
> but fundamentally it was a matter of taste
> > Yes taste
> that commands us to get out to make a wry face draw
> > out a sneer
> even if for this the precious capitol of the body the
> > head
> > > must fall

It is striking to find poets who have endured social
and political oppression or witnessed the Holocaust
and who have not tried to exploit these experiences.
In his best poems Herbert makes us read beneath the
literal level of information because he sets no scene.
You will find no cinematic descriptions of men being
leveled by machine guns or chased down dark alleys.
No spectacles. Herbert trusts his art enough to let the
bloody action occur offstage. Herbert affirms through
negation. How effectively he encompasses the transi-
tion from IS NOT to IS should be clear from the opening lines in a haunting lyric from the Milosz anthology, "Our Fear":

Our fear
does not wear a night shirt

. . .

does not extinguish a candle

does not have a dead man's face either

our fear
is a scrap of paper
found in a pocket
'warn Wójcik
the place on Dluga Street is hot'

The poem embodies history. It has to, and it is through this sense of responsibility to history that the poem derives its tension, threading its way between the pitfalls of overcommitment and aloofness. As a bridge between the void and the world, the poem insures that what is written is not swallowed up. Nowhere does Herbert better focus his consciousness of history as force than in these lines from "The Murderers of Kings":

not one of them managed to change the course of
    history
but the dark message has gone from generation to
    generation
so these small hands are worthy of reflection
small hands in which the certainty of the blow is
    trembling

I doubt that there is an American poet who has not puzzled over the question of what it means to write at peril to one's life and at the same time to write with the knowledge that you are being read, in the wrong way perhaps, but still being read. From Herbert's title poem:

> Too old to carry arms and fight like the others—
>
> they graciously gave me the inferior role of chronicler
> I record—I don't know for whom—the history of the
>   siege
>
> I am supposed to be exact but I don't know when the
>   invasion began
> two hundred years ago in December in September
>   perhaps yesterday at dawn
> everyone here suffers from a loss of the sense of time

Herbert lets us know that he doesn't want to write only about the facts but that history has forced him into this circumstance:

> during elemental
> catastrophes
> the arithmetic
> becomes complicated
>   ("Mr. Cogito on the Need for Precision")

Report from the Besieged City was first published by internees in the Rakowiecka Prison in Warsaw: most of the copies were confiscated.

NEW POEMS: The Other Part (1908), by Rainer Maria
Rilke, translated by Edward Snow.

Rilke has changed alongside our changing lives. He
was in danger of being transformed—especially during the 1960's in America—into a cult figure, a savant,
like Rabindranath Tagore or Kahil Gibran. This is the
Rilke who gave advice, the Rilke of the *Letters to a
Young Poet* and certain passages in his novel, *The Notebooks
of Malte Laurids Brigge*, with his injunctions about what
you must do "for the sake of a single poem": "You
must understand animals, must feel how birds fly, and
know the gesture which small flowers make when they
open in the morning. . . . You must also have been
beside the dying." I once heard an undergraduate remark wistfully, "Oh, I went through a big Rilke phase
and can't read him anymore." Rilke is a poet who gives
people strength at certain points in their lives, and after that they can't return to him because, I am convinced, they went to him for the wrong reasons.

Several translations that have appeared over the last
ten years, especially those by Edward Snow, Stephen
Mitchell, Rika Lesser, David Young and Robert Bly,
have helped to alter this. With a discriminating intelligence, they achieve the balance of intellect and passion necessary to recapture this poet's dialectic of the
vast and the small: uncontrollable distances, the wind
full of infinite space, and the things that belong to the
child's world—puppets, toys, marionettes. These translations

have brought Rilke back, if not from the land of the dead, at least from the realm of the misconstrued. They have restored him to his works.

And from the gardens

> the summer hangs like a heap of marionettes,
> headfirst, exhausted, done in.
> But from the ground, out of old forest skeletons,
> volition rises:
> ("Late Autumn in Venice")

Both volumes of *New Poems* are more down-to-earth than the rest of Rilke's work. The Rilke of *New Poems* is not the superspiritual Rilke of *The Book of Hours*, or the yearning, cosmic Rilke of the *Duino Elegies*, or the Rilke who sought the invisible through sound in the *Sonnets to Orpheus*. The specious philosophy falls by the wayside. The Rilke of *New Poems: The Other Part*, influenced by his contact with Cézanne and Rodin, is still tougher-minded, more severe. If the first volume of *New Poems* aspires to transcendence, the second, with its stress on deaths and disappearances, is geared toward survival. In these works, Rilke opposed not only his own inclinations but also the burgeoning interest in psychoanalysis and the unconscious. He didn't want answers to his problems but ways to work, "equivalents in the visible world for what you had seen inside."

He found what he needed to raid the knowable through the visual in the examples of Cézanne and Rodin. His prose on both men serves as a parallel text to these poems. In *Letters on Cézanne*, Rilke insists that we should learn to look at things as if no own had ever looked at them before. He says of Cézanne's work: "It's as if every place were aware of all the other places." And one hears this insight amplified, transformed, in the poem "Archaic Torso of Apollo": "for there is no place/ that does not see you. You must change your life." He recognizes that Cézanne's swerving from Impressionism required a return to reality. In a foreshadowing of the *Sonnets to Orpheus*, he observes that Cézanne knows how to cast the "loudness of lemons and apples . . . Into a listening blue, as if into an ear, so that it receives a silent response from within."

From Rodin, for whom he worked as a secretary, he acquired a disciplined approach to his own working methods. "Work all the time," Rodin enjoined, "and begin with a trip to the zoo!" And his secretary listened. He tried to write as a painter paints: in front of a model. When the word "experiment" is used of Anglo-American poetry, it usually refers to technique. Rilke's experiment is more radical and fundamental: he translates seeing into being. Many of the poems are about single encounters, snapshots of the soul seen with the stranger's alert gaze. They are all eye and no I, and yet the first person pronoun is always implicit.

"The Panther," one of the most dynamic of the *New Poems*, was the first poem to emerge from this enterprise. With panthers on the brain (after having seen a Greek statue of one in Rodin's studio), Rilke went to the zoo. The resulting poem moves from contemplation of the creature as a work of art to the creature itself:

> From time to time the curtain of the pupils
> silently parts—. Then an image enters,
> goes through the taut stillness of the limbs,
> and is extinguished in the heart.

Similarly, *New Poems: The Other Part* begins with an object from the ancient world. "Archaic Torso of Apollo," like all ruins, is the sum of its missing parts. The imagination supplies the wholeness. Reality doesn't disappoint but rather elevates through its incompleteness: "We never knew his head . . . But/his torso still glows." As in Cézanne's still lifes, there is nothing static in the *New Poems* because the perceived object becomes subject as well and looks back at the perceiver:

> she turns her face straight into your own:
> and you unexpectedly meet your gaze
> in the yellow amber of her round eye-stones:
> closed in like some long-extinct insect.
> ("Black Cat")

Rilke looks at things like a lover who simultaneously woos and holds the beloved at arm's length, reserving the right to depart when the poem ends, often after a sonnet's predetermined number of lines, lest he be swallowed up:

> As you walk along,
> a swarm of gnats moves with you, as though
> behind your back everything were being
> instantly annihilated and erased.
> ("The Parks")

Another moment of true feeling occurs in the brave, mysterious "Encounter on the Chestnut Avenue," a little known but major poem. Here, in an explosion of desire, the boundary between self and other is shattered.

whitely a solitary shape
flared up, long remaining distant
and then finally, the downdriving light
boiling over it at every step,

bearing on itself a bright pulsation,
which in the blond ran shyly to the back.
But suddenly the shade was deep,
and nearby eyes lay gazing

from a clear new unselfconscious face,
which, as in a portrait, lived intensely
in the instant things split off again:
first there forever, and then not at all.

If Rilke is the nonpossessive and nonpossessable lover,
he is also our great poet of childhood. Destiny, he em-
phasized, is no more than what's packed into childhood, which exists for him, along with animals (his
"creature world") and flowers in a realm of pure duration, where things are as aware of the world as they
are unaware of death. But as an adult, Rilke needed
death to free himself from self-consciousness. Death's
presence, he wrote, can release us from our "anxious"
striving "to please . . . so that for a while we act life/
transported, not thinking of applause." His dead like
being dead, but they have to labor hard for a taste of
eternity. Eurydice in "Orpheus. Eurydice. Hermes" doesn't
want to come up from the underworld, and the refrain for her desirable state, "uncertain, gentle, and
without impatience," is as apt as it is lovely. In "Portrait of My Father as a Young Man" Rilke sees himself
in the process of dying, even if his hands are fading
away more slowly than his father's photograph. His

own "Self-Portrait From the Year 1906" is as wide-awake, as purged of vanity as Cézanne's, and has the same mixture of detachment and involvement, the "matter-of-fact interest of a dog who sees himself in a mirror and thinks: there's another dog." Looking "death in the face" was good practice for looking at life.

Rilke was always "secretly departing" and regarded a posture of departure as an inescapable sign of our own awareness of our own mortality. What could be more like a lover's discourse than his poems, so full of longing and so apprehensive of its realization? Rilke loathed possession. Interested only in pursuit, he wanted to control his relationships with others. When anyone tried to draw too close, he withdrew. Paula Modersohn Becker suffered his cold shoulder when she left her husband and came to Paris to establish herself as an artist. Only after her early death would Rilke try to justify his aloofness, with some of his most searing lines, both lament and lesson, in "Requiem for a Friend" (as translated by Stephen Mitchell):

> We need, in love, to practice only this:
> letting each other go. For holding on
> comes easily; we do not need to learn it.
>
> . . .
>
> For somewhere there is an ancient enmity
> between our daily life and the great work.
> Help me, in saying it, to understand it.

Rilke stands very close in spirit to American transcendentalists like Emerson and Thoreau but, unlike them, he worked out his vision in an urban atmosphere, among derelicts and corrupted objects: musty zoos, carousels, and parks where parrots "chew a gray something, find it tasteless, toss it away." While T.S. Eliot, in poems written just after *New Poems*, was revolted by the images of death and sensuality he witnessed in London streets, Rilke is shattered but accepting. He retrieves what others discard. He neither recoils at the sight of corpse being washed nor shrinks from the anonymous dead body's power to make the washers pay heed to death, so that the "one without names/lay there bare and clean and issued laws." Though he lacks a sense of humor, his refusal to take refuge in irony is one of his most appealing traits. Rilke, stalking Paris in the August heat, is like the panther, glaring out from behind the bars of his cage. His work is wrested from a menacing indifference at the world's heart. With his wild energy and awed, rapt gaze, he synthesizes impulses in Baudelaire and Whitman. He is a man of the crowd who is not swallowed up by the crowd; he finds an identity, a wholeness, in being a stranger.

New Poems: The Other Part reminds us that sensitivity, receptiveness and listening are not contrary to toughness of mind, that the violence of our insights is what we need to begin to praise. And praising is what in the end came to matter most for Rilke: "But this can still be kept a secret: how good the grass is and how soft." His growth as a poet was in learning how not be consumed, how not to fear abandon, how not to confuse loss with annihilation, and in recognizing that the turmoil of his calling would only leave him alone at great risk. His work tells us that we are solitary by nature but that absence is not loss, that in forever taking leave, we encounter being.

From the Desert to the Book: Dialogues with Marcel Cohen, translated by Pierre Joris, and *The Book of Shares,* by Edmond Jabès, translated by Rosmarie Waldrop.

Edmond Jabès is an Egyptian Jew. Forced to leave Cairo during the Suez crisis in 1956, he moved to Paris and several years later exploded with *The Book of Questions.* He was physically untouched by the Holocaust and considers that his own situation in Egypt paralleled that of the American Jew. He feels himself to be everywhere an outsider on many counts: as an exile and a Jew, and as one who writes in French, outside his own language.

From the Desert to the Book: Dialogues with Marcel Cohen and *The Book of Shares,* are summations, distillations of the messages in the "empty envelope" of his massive, polyphonic *Book of Questions.*

Mr. Jabès, who was first brought to wide attention by Jacques Derrida, is one of the most quotable of writers. "It is only in the desert, in the dust of our words, that the divine word could be revealed. A nakedness, a transparency of the world we have to recover each time if we are to preserve the hope of speaking. Wandering creates the desert." A dialogue is maintained in the desert, at the point where the horizon becomes visible. "The horizon exaggerates the nearness of the horizon." But he is, in the end, unquotable, because each interjection, each interruption—and it is interruptions which comprise the body of his texts—is a question that creates another rupture. Words are nomads: they move on and on, with trepidation.

Despite its subtitle, *From the Desert to the Book* bears little resemblance to a standard interview with a writer. It is both a superb introduction to his work and a final—clear yet elusive—statement. There is no small talk. The interview, according to the writer Marcel Cohen, is "neither completely written nor completely oral. Its form is rather that of notes which participants at a public meeting pass back and forth when they can't and won't just talk or just write."

*

The book consists mostly of abstract discourse about Mr. Jabès' metaphysics of becoming, broken, from time to time, by mention of things that helped form him. He tells of friendships and work habits and experiences: how Max Jacob taught him to be *"different"* (does Jabès echo Derrida or Derrida Jabès?); how he wrote *The Book of Questions* while going to and from work on the Paris Metro; how he would take a blanket and go alone into the Egyptian desert for days. These "experiences" are highlighted by their infrequency: they do not make up the body of the book. Jabès does his reader a service when he draws our attention to the role of the body in writing, just as he once did when, in an earlier interview, he talked about the profound effect his asthma had on his process of composition.

The Book of Shares, superbly translated by Rosmarie Waldrop, reads like a purely aphoristic distillate of Mr. Jabès' earlier books: his voice refining, retrying many of the propositions he introduced in them. He belongs

in the spiritual company of Kafka and Beckett. They
inhabit the same no-place, which is everywhere, creating works which miraculously cleave to the essential
while avoiding the generic. This is man stripped of
everything but voices, some eloquent, some strangu-
lated. Writing, for Mr. Jabès, is an "audible silence."

Jabès' work, already dry, would be arid were it nor
for his passion and desperate urgency. His is an art of
angular thrusts, of juxtapositions carried to such an
extreme that you can hear the scream at its center: the
voice of the Holocaust, of the unredeemed and the un-
redeemable. It is an art of incantation, ablaze with
inner fire, consuming itself. "To introduce autobiography into a Jewish text, to rehabilitate the I—the particular that gives rise to the universal—to insist on the
face and then proceed slowly to wipe out this insistence."

Mr. Jabès broaches the question of how to write after the Holocaust, long after Wittgenstein wrote his
famous conclusion to the *Tractatus Logico-Philosophicus*,
tormenting us with tautology: "What we cannot speak
about we must pass over in silence." (That "what" is
like something you know is there but cannot touch.) It
is as if history, diabolically, had got inside the universal mind of philosophy and tampered with the dynamic
inner mechanism. Mr. Jabès has chosen to speak about
something which must remain unspoken, a historical
cataclysm that dismantles writing, since there is no way
through language to get at the heart of evil embodied
by the Holocaust. His imagination is perched on a precipice
of doubt. Still, he must answer to catastrophe and ex-
termination. To resolve the paradox, to speak about that
before which we must remain silent, he poses questions.
We hear isolated voices speak and then disappear, only

to be replaced by further—unanswerable—questions. The voices replace but do not cancel each other.

Much of the dialogue in *From the Desert to the Book* circles around the text of *The Book of Questions*, providing a framework within which to gain access to that book. Even though it appeared in English about twenty years after it was published in France, *The Book of Questions* still seemed like something new. No one had mixed poetry and prose, aphorism and dialogue, in quite this way. The book is feverous and sporadic; it lurches and twists like the rhythm of the Metro, the rhythm of movement and arrested movement: the text parallels and reflects the stops and starts, the waiting, the apprehension, the anticipation, of this daily travel, travail. I love the rapidity with which Jabès leaps from the cabala to the voices of imaginary rabbis like a midrash, to the central characters, the lovers Sarah and Yukel, to the interlocutor, the invisible interrogator. It reminds me of the way William Carlos Williams wrote *Paterson* jotting down lines of poetry on prescription pads between house calls he made in his rounds as a physician. "Every book may finally be only the reflection of its method! It is thus completely natural that *The Book of Questions* is made up of breaks, of interruptions," Mr. Jabès says; continuity should be disrupted. The text devours itself and spews out another text. The text erases itself and we're left with this white space whose margins Jabès loves: silence, blankness, the desert; waiting. He reduces the written to a mark instead of a word to make lack visible: a dot, an empty envelope. "The writer does not try to be the witness. He is only there listening to the words that trace his future."

It's not that there is no story, no narrative, but that for Mr. Jabès the story is implicit. He gives us the scaffolding and the threshold so we can imagine the frame and the dwelling. "As far as the story of Sarah and Yukel is concerned," he says regarding the central characters in *The Book of Questions*, "there was no need to tell it. That's why it remains so fragmentary. Their personal biography is so crushed by the scope of the historical drama—the murder of six million men, women and children—that it cannot reflect it at all. That's exactly why their story is given only in small fragments. *One needs only a few markers to recognize a path*" (italics mine).

Mr. Jabès is an epic minimalist, using the sparest of means to suggest a vast horizon of dialogue, a chorus of invisible voices. When a writer like Paul Celan or Mr. Jabès employs surrealist and modernist techniques, he is not making a stylistic decision; it is not a game. There is something glorious, even heroic, about the purity of Jabès' integrity and ambition, which reminds me, in its relaxed, yet muscular, strenuousness, of George Oppen's later poetry. He submerges the reader in a hail of aphorisms, which have a compelling violence of thought. With each echo of a prior word, the dialectic splinters into many dialogues.

He is difficult, not impenetrable, and the effect of reading him is bracing, like time spent in the desert. "The questioning has created emptiness. This emptiness was needed so that a new interrogation—virgin, free—may see the light of day." The dialogues make clear his hope that men will "know how to find dignity in the imbalance of the question and no longer in an answer that paralyzes both him and us."

If your personality is a field, then the coexistence of mul-
tiple personalities is not carried on as a split. The minute
you have a split then you have another kind of Other . . .
And speaking for myself, I call the unconscious the Other.
All the other others are integrated.   —*Robert Duncan*

Some months ago, after weeks of unending rain, when dreams of drowning were not dreams, the sun broke through at dusk. I walked out into an evening ripe with twittering. Sound of a chainsaw somewhere in a house under construction. I could not stop walking. An Irish setter seemed to dissolve into the glow of the fields, a coppery haze. The word crepuscular came to mind. And so did the work of Robert Duncan. "Often I am permitted to return to a meadow . . ."

> It is only a dream of the grass blowing
> east against the source of the sun
> in an hour before the sun's going down.

It is the time of day that signifies return. I cannot count the times I have emerged from the subway to see the facades of warehouses glow, and the surface of the Hudson turn to quicksilver, and the day's chaos fade.

I found myself thinking about the word crepuscular and the evening light I walked in just north of Albany at the end of a rain-sodden April when I could not count on the fingers of one hand the number of times the sun had raised its head. The stillness and sharp

fading light quieted me and reminded me of the way
Duncan stays with a theme, hovering, proceeding, but
not necessarily forward, his peculiar steadiness of rhythm
not to be mistaken for monotony, the emotional drive
behind the cadence. But I am thinking of evening—
and the warring elements within the self. The bent bow
quivers when the arrow is let go. Listen to this passage from that rending, utterly destroying series of "Passages," *Tribunals*, from which we cannot return to the
world unchanged.

> Out of the sun and the dispersing stars,
>   go forth the elemental sparks,
>   outpouring vitalities,
> stir in the *Salitter* of the earth
>   a *living* Spirit,
> and the stars, mothers of light, remain,
>   having each
> its own "organic decorum, the complete
> loyalty of a work of art to a shaping
>   principle
>   within itself"—
>
>   ("Passages 31: The Concert")

A landscape of disproportions timed to the mind's drift.
A mental world made physical. Romantic, expansive.
Horizontal, like a field. Make Believe. Making belief.
What is is. And is about to be.

*

I want to talk about Robert Duncan's gesture, the
open field whose energies he engenders, the line, breath,
space, spacing, the placement of words on the page,
seeing double. My talking about the rain and times of

day is not an evasion. The poems inspire meditation. The words move me toward the world, toward what is going on around me, where poetry that is more descriptive usurps the existence of the things it names, takes their place, like a franchise or other products of advanced capitalism. As he has said, "As a matter of principle I don't understand that anything in writing is prohibited. Like what if it were sloppy." He writes against closure, towards openness, toward—being toward. His project is a way of showing how much poetry, how much of creation, is about "a way" of going on. Of creating meaning. It is like walking in a field where jet trails take the place of clouds overhead, a fire rages, frogs croak, naked bodies cavort: an odd assemblage.

Unlike the dramatic lyric in which the poem links up to a particular event, and unlike the poetry of the self or voice, the drama here is life as experience in language commensurate with consciousness; and lyrical events occur within the body of the poem as part of being—all of the selves in the "selva oscura" projected outward.

> For now in my mind all the young men of my time
> have withdrawn allegiance from *this world*, from
> public things •
>
> and their studies in irreality deepen,
>
> industries, businesses, universities, armies
>
> shudder and cease
>
> so that the stone that comes into being

when the pupil of the eye that like a moon
takes all seeing from an unseen sun's light
reflected makes
held under his tongue each man speak
wonders to come.

Chaos/and the divine measures and orders

so wedded are

we have but to imagine

ourselves the Lover

and the Beloved appears
("Passages 27: Transgressing the Real")

Certain works of art capture the feeling of a generation. *Bending the Bow* is one of these.

*

When I look at Robert Duncan's work on the page another image comes to mind: the DNA molecule. I think of thoughts that aren't expressible in conventional, ready-made syntax, the way the words are placed on the page, like a map of the brain. This feeling is reaffirmed by his statement: "Meaningfulness is intent . . . I don't believe there is any chance at all." (Dante says, "I would press the juice out of my conception." Nothing [unless everything!] is random in Dante.) This is what Duncan is getting at when he quotes John Adams as saying "Let the human Mind loose . . . It must be loose.//It will be loose." *(Passages 32)*

The key to Duncan's work, if such a thing exists, is in the same passage, another quotation, from John Adams,

"Marginalia to Court de Gebelin's *Monde Primitif*":

Something mysterious, however, under all this.

He conveys this through the voice, the actual words, of John Adams, jotted down in an unselfconscious moment, unintended for the eyes of others. This can be assumed through its status as marginalia. Imagine a poet's life-work as marginalia: his real thoughts, against the ones he puts forth publicly tempered by a stance, a mask— the human mind let loose! Freed from the strictures of the will and the screen images of voluntary memory. Imitating the structure of the universe, or if not, consuming itself with that which it was nourished by rather than expiring, naturally, in time. Duncan's concern for the truth is paramount because he believes that the myth already is—beyond our willing. The will is not volitional. The premise that underlies his work is that "We have come so far that all the old stories/whisper once more./ Mount Segur, Mount Victoire, Mount Tamalpais . . . " ("A Poem Beginning With A Line By Pindar") with the latter "Mount" pointing toward an indigenous tradition.

> It is as if I were moving towards
> the wastes of water all living things remember the
>   world to be,
> the law of me
>   going under the wave.
> ("In Place of A Passage 22")

Duncan's openness, his process of writing, has to do with gaps—space, spaces that are left for the Other to fill, as he says in "An interlude of rare beauty": "Naming/

no more than our affection for naming." His gesture generates a movement in me toward the possibility that experience has meaning, that I can grasp, without pinions, this instant, this hour, this turn of events, even, though not yet, this chatter—heard everywhere— that consumes so much life and time. Why does so strenuous, though not strained, an act of mind remind me that I live in my body? It has to do with the act of thou-ing another being, and the exorcism of negative forces—often through homage, as in the passages that derive from John Adams. Or constellated rage. Outcry without rhetoric: by staying with the line—

> in every party partisans of the torment,
>   Tyranny throws up from its populace a
>   thousand
> tyrant-faces, seethes and dies down, would-be
> administrators of the evil or challengers of the
>   establishment
> seeking their share of the Power. *Se le fazion che porti*
> *non son false...*
>
> but whose face is this face? so many
> having only Hell's loan of a face at interest—
>
> he was but one of the many frogs croaking
> from the desolate marsh, seething, collapsing,
> that they call the Law, figments of the media
>   surrounding them
>
>   ("Passages 35: Before the Judgment")

Poetry, in addition to being what Oscar Milosz called the "passionate pursuit of the real," (and where Duncan is concerned I would emphasize the pursuit), cannot be willed. In Duncan's case it is a kind of hymn or prayer to the involuntary—the image, the rhythm, the cadence, that discovers itself. It comes from the recognition that there is no distinction between the inside and the outside of things when language mediates between them, the language of eyes and lips, not of seeing with the eyes: seeing being one of desire's extensions: we want the things we look at—not the things we see—to become as we are, indelibly, and by putting the moment that cannot recur (however technology chooses to mock this process) into the realm of first priority, Whitehead's "presentational immediacy," we give life to death, presence to absence, fullness to emptiness—in the feeling of being gripped and rent by a woman who catches my eye crossing the street, folding up the sidewalk, a glance that takes everything in, and yet, and then, it dissolves into others. It is the real, essential self freed of habit, of the habit of denial, duty and resignation, like "love at first sight," like everything that happens without the intervention of the will.

> The men are working in the street.
> The sound
>
> of pick and pneumatic drill
>
> punctuates
> the chirrup a bird makes,
>
> a natural will
> who works the tossing dandelion head
>
> —a sheaf of poems.
>
> They are employd

at making up a joyous

possibility.

They are making a living
where I take my life.

("Answering")

The mystery is there, waiting, and the poet is the creature whose life's work it is to surprise, to return to the
world what the world has given. Instances of pure relation! Things do not remain the same while we look
at them, no meaning is fixed outside a given context.

*

Duncan's art is all about how we perceive, how perceptions evolve, and are seized or ignored. The problem, poetically, is that nothing stands still. And yet if
you can get clear—and he often does—there are sources
of inspiration in the constant human crush—once nothing
stands still, once the traffic of bodies is like a wave,
this continual movement is like a vast stillness, crepuscular; but if I am enchanted by the cheekbones and
Botticellian aura of a woman across from me on the
crosstown bus; if I am gripped by the urge to recapture this intense timeless timebound feeling in words,
I balk at the thought of reducing another person to
the nonstatus of an object. It is necessary to oppose
vision to the prevailing surfaces—(masks of faces)—
that disguise themselves as reality, "having only Hell's
loan of a face at interest," when reality stands apart
from pavements, machinations, and video screens: and
without feeling, reality becomes unreal. The intersec-
tion of time and the timeless is the crossroad at which

we forever find—uncover—poetry and the lack of frequency of this conjunction is to be marvelled at.

*

If we knew what beheld us!

*

Poetry tells what we have lived, how we have felt, and where we can audibly vent our darkness, and is accountable to history. Duncan quotes Whitman in *Passages 26*: "The Soldiers," as saying "*'The United States themselves are essentially the greatest poem'?*" throwing in that question mark to disrupt our comfort. Awareness will disturb your sleep. Contradictions are not intended to be resolved. And we cannot cavil our way through this impasse. It is an awakening we crave, and the poem responds to the desire, to essential desire, to desire as essence—desire, it seizes what it sees. Sexual at root, it pervades us as sensual beings. Bootless, unbolted. "For poetry," as Duncan says in *Passages 10*, "is a contagion" and "The ear/catches rime like pangs of disease from the air."

*

In a time such as this one (six months into 1983)—with its ubiquitous return to "form"—another of Duncan's bardic statements in *The Truth and Life of Myth* takes on a new layer of meaning:

> In periods of the greatest panic, such as the eighteenth century following the nightmare religious enthusiasms and wars of the seventeenth, the form tolerable to convention can shrink to a tennis court.

*

America, the American language and landscape. So much of this country, even the hirsute wilderness, is a double of Europe, and the ancient world. Towns with names like Babylon, Athens, Cairo, Attica . . .

> Weavers, potters and carpenters appear to be tribal
>   foreigners . . .
> The Bethlehem Steel Company now in the place
> of the Moravian smithy at Bethlehem

Duncan is not what you'd call a "visual" poet. His writing does not often conjure images in the mind, except through sound, through melopeia, upon reflection, as in the later "Passages" where his chant surrounds the war in Vietnam,

> Mao's own mountain of murdered men,
>
> the alliteration of ems like Viet Nam's
>
> burnd villages . . .

Duncan's voice is in the sound of the words, not in the literal world they invoke. Reading him is like watching a silent film such as Carl Dreyer's *Joan of Arc*: it is all close-ups and the pathos is so immense and grandiose and unabashed I feel torn between laughter and tears. The sublime always hangs on the precipice of the ridiculous. The form itself is an exorcism, and the outburst, tearing open the air with a sound the ears cannot register, hears. It is what I referred to before as the emotional drive of the cadence that gives these words the gravity they have, their power to stick in the mind, in spite of the facility of the wordplay. This is something I want to return to. Writing and truth. The necessary connection. Not the superficies of form and content, or mode.

All endings, other than death, are provisional. And there is no reason to speak of the aesthetic "object." And the creative will is not experienced as force. And the mind is keen on seeking.

> Child of a century more skeptic than
>   unbelieving,   adrift
> between two contrary educations,
>
> that of the Revolution, which disowns
>   everything,
> and that of the Reaction,
> which pretends to bring back the ensemble
>   of Christian beliefs,
>
> will I find myself traind to believe
>   everything
>
> as our fathers, the scientists, have been
>
>   traind to deny?
>
>   ("Passages 32")

This majestic poem aspires to commerce with the infinite, and does not apologize for its spiritual ambition.

> I saw
>
> willingly the strain of my heart break
>   and pour its blood thundering at the life-locks
>
> to release   full   my man's share of the stars'

majesty thwarted.

("Passages 31: The Concert")

The process of writing is linked to our passage through life. We live in passageways and who can retain more than passages of any poet's work, of any piece of music, of life as it is lived or in the process of being remembered. "Passages." I am so often forced, through circumstances, as now to think and write while in passage, pausing beside a streetlight to get down a sentence. Passages are what we seek for and what we are left with.

The evening, lingering, the light going on long after the sun has gone down. Intense, diffuse.

Generative themes. Being called, listening. Shaping. In a season of so much rainfall it is to be hoped that other—inner— reservoirs are full.

A fantasia. Sage business, "resonances of meaning exceeding what we/understand." An ascending voice, wild with desire. The pain of intermediate steps, hesitations, transitional phases. The letter e. Eye.

> The "I" passing into sIght
> the Mind   wherever
>   it touches   blindly

> forming this eye at the boundary it knows

> the brain's ocular stalk inciting
> "that skin, as though it knew and sympathized"

("Passages 33, iv")

A revolutionary, forward surging, thoughtful art. Bookish,

learned, arcane, he is careful, not cautious. Vortex and compost,
energies surge. Staying with what is fleeting.

> a Protestant dynamic!   the line
>
> a trial, each element a crisis of attention
>   yet—"
>   ("Passages 33, v")

Desire creates its own objects. But the quest for the
object of desire is still consuming. "There appeared to
him such a one as he hunted for."

In the poem, in "Passages," Johnson and Dante, Vietnam
and Malebolge, can have it out. The poet becomes the
only acknowledged "legislator of the world." This seems
delusionary and phantasmagoric until you read it; then,
as history recedes like ticker tape and piles up in the
basement, what the poem, "Passages," offers comes forward.

> Discontent with that first draft, where one's own
>   hatred enters   Hell   gets out of hand
>
> again and again Virgil   ever standing by Dante
>   must caution him   —in Malebolge
>
> where the deep violence begins
>
>   ***
>
> destroyers of cities and orders
>
> . . . their faces,names . . . Rubins, Hayakawas,
>   Aliotos, Reagans, Nixons
>
>   as we go upward the stupidity thickens,

> reflections in the oil slick multiplied.

("Passages 35: Before the Judgement")

Duncan explores the tragic possibilities in the common fracture of reality. The "real" is unequivocal, a gnattering fact. The social changes in our time are like a wound that hasn't knit and makes us uneasy. He perceives war as the extension of thwarted, and consequently destructive, energies. As Dante says, "to describe the bottom of the whole universe is not an enterprise to be take up in sport, nor for a tongue that cries mamma and daddy." And it is tragic when the warring elements, within the self and the body politic, their transit blocked, seek an outlet, a way into the world, in war—a way of scratching an itch guaranteed to draw blood and increase desperation—(the Vietnamese mosquito proved as hard to subdue as the Viet Cong).

> . . . the all-American boy in the cockpit
> loosing his flow of napalm, below in the jungles
> "any life at all or sign of life" his target, drawing now
> not with crayons in his secret room

and then, devastatingly, jetting fire—

> the burning of homes and the torture of mothers and
> fathers and children,
> their hair a-flame, screaming in agony, but

> in the line of duty, for the might and enduring fame
> of Johnson, for the victory of American will over its
> victims,
> releasing his store of destruction over the
> enemy,

in terror and hatred of all communal things, of
    communion,
        of communism •

    ("Passages 25: Up Rising")

  Duncan doesn't hedge—risks the bold statement and,
in our time, his refusal to take refuge in irony is an
incalculable grace.

                                *

  This is poetry without concession. Against the tyranny of subject matter. Much of the pathos in Duncan's
poetry comes from his struggle between ways of telling, a struggle between story, narrative, and open form.
How can there be pathos in this unspoken dialectic?
Because story is tied to tradition, in the largest and
most primal sense, that connects the poet to the human community, and tradition, in the process of im-
peding progress, consoles. Myth intersects with history. His art is not an art of hurry.

        Solitary first riders advance into legend.

      This land, where I stand, was all legend
    in my grandfathers' time: cattle raiders,
        animal tribes, priests, gold.
    It was the West. Its vistas painters saw
        in diffuse light, in melancholy,
    in abysses left by glaciers as if they had been the sun
        primordial carving empty enormities
                    out of the rock.

                    Snakes lurkd
          guarding secrets. Those first ones
                      survived solitude.

    ("A Poem Beginning With A Line by Pindar")

Duncan will set out as though he wanted to tell a story and be undone—productively—by distractions—interruptions. Other priorities impinge. And so he asks us to pay attention to the teller, to what he calls "the fiction of what man is." Too often the story, or tale, or narrative is mistaken for linear telling, where the point is to preserve the effect: "Only connect."

> Coming across an old photograph of him
>   no recognition stirs,   his time
> that was forever has slipt away.
> The key of C minor no longer belongs to
>   the song I have forgotten and will never
> sing•   the longing, the lingering
>   tune of it
>
>   ("Passages 16: The Currents")

The further away in time we move from the events themselves the more opaque and mysterious these details become. The fabric of history is myth. Information is digested. Only shimmering instants wait to be plucked, impossibly (always threatening to dissolve, as though one and one were one, not two) from windows.

> The secret! the secret! It's hid
>   in its showing forth.
>
>   ("Passages 2: At the Loom")

It would be a mistake to read Duncan's poetry more for its manner than its matter. It would be wrong to underestimate the persistence of non-meaning in the succession of instants, which is why poetry wanders, why it is so intent on tracking the mind's movement,

from the sound of a basketball dribbled in the courtyard now to Ralph Kirkpatrick on the harpsichord, translating the silence of Scarlatti's notes into sound—nor was
there any way, or any reason, to escape the sultriness
of the day, lingering, in the city, hanging like breath,
among the leaves in the trees lining the avenues, as if
they had been placed there for this reason, like hidden illuminations.

Where else does he lead but to that no place—that
State of Mind called awareness of death. (Listen to the
pathos in the scraping shuffling sound of invisible others
around you now.)

> The hosts have gone down to the edge of the sea,
>   time has swept their tents away.
>
> The air we breathe grows dark with the debris of
>   burning fats
>   and dense with animal smoke.   All day
>
> exhausts pour forth into the slues of night their
>   centuries,
>   the black soil scums the putrid bay,
>
> the light is acrid to our eyes, and all the old runes
>   thicken in our minds—
>
> Ge stinks to Heaven from the dumps of sleep.
>
> ("Passages 34: The Feast")

Duncan is saved from pretentiousness by his interest, his probing mind, and by caring, exploring the
possibility that we might find meaning in the connections, links and parallelisms that exist in texts as much

as they exist in nature or in the mind. But both he and
Pound place too much weight or value on the cultural
hierarchy they invoke through their allusions. Is the
mention of Hermes Trismegistes of a higher order than
any other proper name independent of context? Sometimes the streets of the imagination here are too lined
with Persian carpets for passage. We want to linger
and don't want to track the mud from our boots across
the figures in the carpets.

There is an absence of the present in much of Duncan's
work, which is rooted in the distant past and the ap-
prehended future. Notice how rarely we know where
he physically is, how little weather there is in his work—
as if he and the physical world were not contiguous—
against the groundings in the classics, myths and texts.
It is too "cosmic." And makes me grateful for a moment such as this one in "Empedoklean Reveries" when
he addresses his cat, sighs, lights a cigarette, comes to
himself.

> I have tamed the Lion Roar.
> It will no longer use me.
>
> Orlando, felix, my little household   relative of the
>   Lion,
> I will remember to pet you;
>   Death takes his time with us.
>
> Long the sexual uproar dies away in me.
>
> Lighting a cigarette. Coming to ourselves.
> From long ago   ceremonies of burning and smoking.
>
> I have burnd the Lion in his own fire.

The Lioness rages in the hunting field
far from where we are.

Because of what we love   we are   increasingly at
    War.
        That Sphere of all Attractions   draws us from
    what we are.—

The connection between perceptions is analogical. Keeping
the spectre in sight, remembering, as Walter Benjamin
says in his essay on Leskov, "The Storyteller," that "Death
is the sanction of everything that the storyteller can
tell. He has borrowed his authority from death . . .
Death appears (in a story by Hebel) . . . with the same
regularity as the Reaper does in the processions that
pass around the cathedral clock at noon." Teaching us
to meet the world with courage, cunning, and high
spirits.

*

I remember passages in Duncan's poems more than
I remember poems, with the significant exceptions of
"A Poem Beginning With A Line By Pindar," "Essay
at War" (from *Derivations*), and "My Mother Would
Be A Falconress." These leave an imprint on my mind
where the bulk of the work leaves an impression. Sometimes
there is a blurring of the poem, not wheel-spinning in
the pejorative sense, but preparation, ritual. I say this
while knowing that this criticism of his work is built
into its structure—and into my own sense of that structure
as a map of the mind—but we owe it to the poetry to
notice when our attention flags as much as when it's
engaged.

*

It is not possible to perceive the truth without terror, yet it doesn't kill you, terror, only death does that.
(As X said of a beautiful woman, "She only looks in-
vulnerable. She must be trembling inside, like the rest
of us."—Not that X trembled all that visibly. . . .)

*

Another evening—the other side of the crepuscular—
sun-lost, blinded by the lightning that took so many
snapshots just north of Albany, booming, scalding, scanning the distances, a house how many miles away, a
man, a woman, at a window, quietly, far off—consoled
by the calmness other people possess—or seem to from
the outside.

*

The mind grasps at signs, but it is the heart that
longs to read meaning—into—to animate the inanimate—
to imprint the universal void with its literal impression. And the creative voice recapitulates the Creation.
Duncan's writing, his prose as well as his poetry, is a
meditation on the poet's work, his free labor, the pleasure that grows in the process that only recognizes
itself once it is set going. But he too must draw blood
to break free, take on identity, as he makes clear in
what may be his finest poem and—to risk hyperbole—
one of the great poems of the century, "My Mother
Would Be A Falconress."

> Ah, but high, high in the air I flew.
> And far, far beyond the curb of her will,
> were the blue hills where the falcons nest.
> And then I saw west to the dying sun—
> it seemd my human soul went down in flames.
> I tore at her wrist, at the hold she had for me,
> until the blood ran hot and I heard her cry out,

far, far beyond the curb of her will·

to horizons of stars beyond the ringing hills of the
   world where the falcons nest
I saw, and I tore at her wrist with my savage beak.

Duncan's work is all about this, how desire is manifest in the hand that presses the pen against the paper, how it manifests itself as attention, the scale of things, how the mind-body feels in the space it inhabits; how longing sings, singes, knocks us down and rouses us from torpor—and how our language, bodied forth, tragically, is all that will last.

So it is not by knowledge or learning but by Love
and by Your leave my Lady that we yielded to that
archaic device of personifications, that we began to
see (wraiths out of their capitalizations) three maidens and to hear did we not? the Holy Word—but we
heard Lear also—crying (over 'spilt milk' I said) calling
the lapsed soul. But more—for three maidens were
no wonder—we saw, more substantial, Present, Past
and Future, images not sensible but imagined, bogus eternities of the poetic mind.

(Robert Duncan, Derivations)

day draws near
another one
do what you can
               –Czeslaw Milosz

A specificity that marks time is a form of consolation.
When I looked up at the great digital clock the other
night and saw 5:40 and 70° I thought the world is not
so bad—the time *is* and the temperature's temperate.
Yesterday, in a state of blurry exhaustion from the week,
I took the day off, and wandered the avenues in the
autumn light with my friend Michael Flanagan, a painter
of dream-engendered, precisionist landscapes. After lunch
we set off to see the Velasquez exhibit at the Met. Walking
down Broadway, we turned left on 94th St. and passed
a street that seemed as green and quiet and domestic
as Hempstead. The leaves were still green on the plane
trees while everywhere else in the city they were beginning to turn.

I was more interested in the landscapes surrounding
Velasquez's figures than the figures themselves. I needed
space in which to meditate. I wasn't in the mood for
the master's rooms and silks, his children robbed of
their childhoods. I needed air. Exited Spain in the 17th
century and walked into France—into the 19th century. And as I walked slowly through the room all I
could think about was light. The light in several early
Monet's seemed to be falling right now; I looked overhead

162

to make sure it was not so, looked for the first time at a painting by Fredric Bazille, "Porte de la Reine," sliver of light running through the slit of a gate to the walled town, radiant old stones—and the relief I felt entering the bright room of Bazille's painting is what I feel picking up a poem by James Schuyler.

There are poets whose work relates to the quiet before or after the storm and those who relate to the turbulence of the storm. James Schuyler is one of the former; he demands peace before he can begin.

> In the quiet spaces between equinoctial gales
> silence sparkles
>   ***
> The sun sits in the sky like a painting of it.
>   ("Just Before Fall")

Poems like this are studies in perception. They focus on the quiet spaces, the interstices, between the turbulence. This is where he allows his perceptions to ripen: it is they that will save him, if anything can. The turmoil is alluded to but it remains distinctly, discreetly offstage, yet very much at the centerless center of his work.

A Schuyler poem appears to begin at a random moment and to evoke the randomness in that moment. With the exception of his long poems, the depths they uncover are of the time that is always the present.

> . . . . Time brings us into bloom and we wait, busy,
>   but wait
> For the unforced flow of words and intercourse and
>   sleep and dreams

> In which the past seems to portend a future which is
>   just more
> Daily life.
>
> ("Hymn to Life")

But that present is imbued with the full contents of one's psychic life. Schuyler subverts his own longing for traditional rhetoric, the tropes of the past. He's utterly without any air of self-importance, pomposity. "Hymn to Life" has fits of grandeur but look how he deflates it in the end: it doesn't resolve, it opens up.

>   Is it for miracles
> We live? I love it when the morning sun lights up my
>   room
> Like a yellow jelly bean, an inner glow. May mutters,
>   "Why
> ask questions?" or, "What are the questions you wish
>   to ask?"

Schuyler's persistent present tense is the inside out of Wordsworth's "spots of time." It means he must relinquish control, submit to chance. The heightened moment attaches to *this* tree, *this* wind, *this* catastrophe, *this* in-between mood, (and our moods, Emerson observed, "do not believe in each other"). Rarely is anything in Schuyler's poetry intended to become emblematic, except to witness that *this* is what moved him to write. "All things are real/no one a symbol" ("Letter to a Friend: Who is Nancy Daum?").

It's always a shock when one has searched for a subject or wondered how to proceed with the next poem to open one of Schuyler's books at any point and read such characteristic lines as these from "June 30, 1974," too long to quote in full:

> Let me tell you
> that this weekend Sunday
> morning in the country
> fills my soul
> with tranquil joy . . .

There's an implicit: "I can breathe now" here.
He eases his way into particulars.

> the dunes beyond
> the pond beyond
> the humps of bayberry—
> my favorite
> shrub (today,
> at least)—are
> silent as a mountain
> range:

And when he leaps, comes up with a wild association—"silent as a mountain/range"—the implication
is "pay no attention, don't stop now, get on to the
next line." His poems give order to an untypical existence painted with love and care. They chronicle time
parceled out.

When Malcolm Lowry describes the Hotel Casino de
la Selva in the opening paragraphs of *Under the Volcano* we know that the present state of the world is
being represented in miniature.

> Palatial, a certain air of desolate splendor pervades
> it. For it is no longer a Casino. You may not even
> dice for drinks in the bar. No one ever seems to swim
> in the magnificent Olympic pool. The springboards

stand empty and mournful. Its jai-lai courts are grass-
grown and deserted. Two tennis courts only are kept
up in the season.

This is precisely the kind of overdetermined significa-
tion you will not find in Schuyler.

Disdaining any serious pose even when in desperate
straights, Schuyler is a master of the light touch, the
gentle nudge. My suffering is nothing, he seems to say,
compared with that which surrounds me.

> My abstention from the park
> is for Billy Nichols who went
> bird-watching there and, for
> his binoculars, got his
> head beat in. Streaming blood,
> he made it to an avenue
> where no cab would pick him up
> *until one did* and at
> Roosevelt Hospital he waited
> several hours before any
> doctor took him in hand. A
> year later he was dead.
> ("Dining Out with Doug and Frank," italics mine)

Many of Schuyler's poems mourn the loss of friends
and the possible loss of friends with mortality impinging.
"Buried at Springs," his elegy for Frank O'Hara, gets
some of its initial power from the echo of "There is a
hornet in the room" with Dickinson's "A fly buzzed
when I died."

Friendship is one of Schuyler's great themes. The Fairfield
Porter episode in "The Morning of the Poem" takes on

a depth and pathos it would not possess if Porter were
alive. The poem becomes a form of healing, of attend-
ing to chaos on the poet's own terms.

There is never an injunction, a stricture imposed. Much
contemporary male poetry seems muscle-bound, alto-
gether armored, compared to Schuyler's. He does not
try to bully the reader into taking a position, except,
as Williams enjoined, to "Make a song out of it." And
that is what Schuyler has done.

> Outside, purple loosestrife
> bloomed in swathes
> that turned the railway ditch and fields into a
> sunset-reflecting lake.
> ("A Few Days")

These days "like any other" also signify the amount of
measured life we are given in our lives like any other
life. But Schuyler's nature is always anthropomorphisized
("The coffee cup has found its way onto the jut of a
crag the size of a foot," "The Edge in the Morning"):
that gradual process provides the poems' movement
from the impersonal to the personal, or vice-versa, and
the reconciliation of the details with the whole provide a kind of argument, the "action" of an exacting—
but never pedantic—intelligence.

> And if you thought March was bad
> Consider April, early April, wet snow falling into
> blue squills
> That underneath a beech make an illusory lake, a
> haze of blue
> With depth to it.
> ("Hymn to Life")

Schuyler's poems are a record of changing skies. The
weather in his poems will not always signify something about relations between the characters, and between the characters and the landscape, and fate. The
weather in Schuyler's poems is a code which says this
much and no more can be salvaged from the wreck-
age. Who needs a larger repertoire than the sun rising
over the bay and dunes and grasses, flowers opening
to first light? "This morning view/is very plain: thou
art/in Heaven:" ("Our Father").

There is no attempt to overwhelm. The emotional pressure
is never in the line itself but diffused gently through
the body of his poems. The awareness of time makes
men tragic. Temporality is pain but to arrest time is
also to limit what sight can harvest.

And Schuyler is sighted. He's amazingly adept at moving
from a flickering surface to an enchanted depth. Look
at this deft chronicle of a sunset.

SONG

The light lies layered in the leaves.
Trees, and trees, more trees.
A cloud boy brings the evening paper:
The Evening Sun. It sets.
Not sharply or at once
a stately progress down the sky
(it's gilt and pink and faintly green)
above, beyond, behind the evening leaves
of trees. Traffic sounds and
bells resound in silver clangs
the hour, a tune, my friend

Pierrot. The violet hour:
the grass is violent green.
A weeping beech is gray,
a copper beech is copper red.
Tennis nets hang
unused in unused stillness.
A car starts up and
whispers into what will soon be night.
A tennis ball is served.
A horsefly vanishes.
A smoking cigarette.
A day (so many and so few)
dies down a hardened sky
and leaves are lap-held notebook leaves
discriminated barely
in light no longer layered.

The complex sonics of "Song" are there in the first two lines, the weighty alliteration of the *l*'s and *t*'s crosscut with rich assonance. What strikes me is the progression from the light curled in the leaves to the leaves of the notebook which must now provide the poem's light. And how the poem moves from labials,"light lies layered", to sibilants, "stately" "sky" "sounds" "resound" "silver", to gutterals, albeit interspersed, "gilt" "green" "grass" "green" "gray," and back again to his lingering *l*'s, duration's darlings—"leaves are lap-held notebook leaves/. . . light no longer layered." "A smoking cigarette" keys us in to the nature of this change. The day is burning down. But note the neutrality of "smoking." (Who is smoking it?) No smoldering, no redness. No portent. Later, a "car" will whisper "into what will soon be night." He shifts into a luxuriant adverbial cluster: "sharply," "stately," "faintly," giving even "sky" the taste of a modifier. He picks up his sound pattern—assonance gaining prominence—

in "beyond, behind the *evening* leaves/of trees." Then
he shifts to internal rhyme, "sounds" "resounds." And
the most telling word play in the poem: the *n* separat-
ing "violet" and "violent." *Violent green* signals a disturbance—a disorder—that will not occupy the poem's
body. No matter how clear—we know what "violent
green" looks like—it is part of the poem's mystery,
like the "smoking cigarette," like the tennis ball that
is served but never returned, like the horsefly who never
was here but who disappears anyway, embodying the
pathos of the vanishing instant. But to touch that violence, which is also the violence of thought, is to have
lived a life.

The sounds work with the sunset, they hesitate, then
surge ahead, just as perception does, in waves. And
the end will affirm what his poems always affirm: that
today is a day like any other. "So much life and never!"
Vallejo wrote. Filled with temporal anguish. For Schuyler
it's the light that allows vision. The self is ancillary to
the light. And the light flows evenly, "no longer layered," depthless, fixed. The day will end as all days
end, in sameness, blurring. And by ending in darkness Schuyler shrewdly reverses the archetype of a poem's
traditional mode of closure.

Schuyler lets us in on the scene of writing, and during
that time he and the poem are as one.

> Enough to
> sit here drinking coffee,
> writing, watching the clear
> day ripen (such
> a rainy June we had)
> while Jane and Joe
> sleep in their room

> and John in his. I
> think I'll make more toast.
> ("June 30, 1974")

The poem happens before anything has happened. It's a celebration of morning, and the pleasures of a solitude you know will be relieved when the "morning of the poem" is over and the proper day begins.

Schuyler's poems narrate many mornings. The morning light. It was the "morning of the poem" for him long before he wrote *The Morning of the Poem*. But morning for Schuyler is also a mourning as "The Edge in the Morning" (too long to quote in full) demonstrates. Here a bravura beginning seems at first to be an inspired parody (in line with Ashbery's "The Skaters") of certain descriptive techniques employed by the "new novel," Roethke's end stopped lines and Whitman's montage in section 15 of "Song of Myself" ("The pure contralto sings in the organ loft/The carpenter dresses his plank . . ."). But Schuyler allows himself no more than a bardic echo. Depth, always questionable, is present here as an absence.

> Walking to the edge with a cup of coffee.
> Sunup.
> The sky is red.
> Sunrise.
> That way, the water is blinding.
> That way, the water is dusted with sleep.

Walking to the edge, he wakes to the edge in the morning to a sense of luminous presences, duplications, and reductions: cup, boat, bone. The bizarre revision—reduction—of "Sunup" to "Sunrise" brings to mind Robbe-Grillet's assertion that there is nothing more fantastic

ultimately than precision. Nothing, I would add, more
ultimately impossible. The edge is the edge of the sublime.
"There are tide lines in the cup."

> The figure of a man turns, steps and bends and draws
>   out of the dishonored and neglected grave cold-
>   blooded fury entrapped in a lobster pot.
>   * * *
> The bay agitatedly tries to smooth itself out.
> If it were tissue paper it would need damp and an
>   iron.
> It is a good deal more than damp.
> What a lot of water.

The images are imbued with an agitation whose emotional source is only revealed at the end when the "I"
enters the poem and replaces the "eye." Before that,
we have this mysteriously precise existential torment.
Water could overwhelm the world or provide a ceno-
taph for Marc Bloch, a French historian killed by the
Nazis. Beyond that, the bay's bereft of "history."

> Suppose I found a bone in the grass and told you it is
>   one of Marc Bloch's?
> It would not be true.
> No it would not be true and the sea is not his grave.
> Noble, great, and good:
> It is his cenotaph.

"The Edge in the Morning" ends as an elegy, ends outside
of the sea's anonymity that threatened to engulf the
poet and the poem.

The Morning of the Poem: It's the press of mortality that
makes the morning the "morning of the poem." The

morning light never hesitates, the body fills up, becomes buoyant with the day. And the afternoon is a
slow and steady emptying. The morning light's an echo
of original light. Schuyler's *in* his poems the way the
action painters wanted to be in their paintings.

Shopping lists and menus are standard fare in modern
poetry, but Schuyler's use of them is poignant, not pointed.
Chance colors his perceptions.

> Hobbled down this everlasting hill to distant
>   Bell's and bought
> Edible necessities: small icy cans of concentrated
>   juice, lemon, lime, orange,
> Vast puffy bags of bread, Smucker's raspberry jam,
>   oatmeal, but not the good,
> The Irish kind (travel note: in New York City you
>   almost cannot buy a bowl
> Of oatmeal: I know I've tried: why bother: it
>   would only taste like paste)
> And hobbled home, studying the for-sale house
>   hidden in scaly leaves
> The way the brownstone facing of your house is
>   coming off in giant flakes
>   ("The Morning of the Poem")

This passage is typical in that it combines several to-
nalities: mild self mockery, delicious Keatsian litany,
"comment," and the image of ruined grandeur.

Schuyler's language is rendered against the idea of depth,
inwardness. He continually verges on the edge of the
sublime. He assigns no importance to anything as such,
merely the diffuse pressure of a life come to be here,
now, inevitably *then*.

A chimney, breathing a little smoke.
The sun, I can't see
making a bit of pink
I can't quite see in the blue.
The pink of five tulips
at five P.M. on the day before March first.
                    ***
It's the yellow dust inside the tulips.
It's the shape of a tulip.
It's the water in the drinking glass the tulips are in.
It's a day like any other.
                    ("February")

The poems have an air of improvisation. Things as they are also means—*not* what they have symbolized. It is as if Schuyler had heeded (and adapted to poetry) Raymond Aron's challenge to Sartre to make philosophy out of a cocktail shaker.

His spontaneity reveals a trust in surfaces. Schuyler knows how to track an image, how to push a surface so that it blossoms into a depth, which is exactly the progression of "The Edge in the Morning." No accident the profusion of flowers in his work. His poems have the intimacy of personal letters (and many are written as such). The risk is always that the poem won't go beyond its premises: his present condition, a feeling, a mood. He is keyed to a moment of pure perception, aura returned to the world.

The plants against the light
which shines in (it's four o'clock)
right on my chair: I'm in my chair:
are silhouettes, barely green,
growing black as my eyes move right,
right to where the sun is.

> I am blinded by a firey circle:
> I can't see what I write.
>   ("Dec. 28, 1974")

When I wonder where I've come across this particular seamless mixture of pure perception and tainted world, high and low tone, lightness and heaviness, this rococo blend of filigree and fire, this brand of deceptive casualness bordering on insouciance, I am taken back to Pushkin in *Eugene Onegin*:

> Your curiosity is burning
> to hear what latest modes require,
> and so, before the world of learning,
> I could describe here his attire;
> and though to do so would be daring,
> it's my profession; he was wearing—
> but *pantaloons, waistcoat,* and *frock,*
> these words are not of Russian stock:

By tainted I mean: mortal. There is tragedy in lightness.

>   Life sends us struggling forth
>   like "the green vine
> angering for life" and rewards us with a plate of
>   popovers labeled "your death."
>   ("A Few Days")

His long poem "A Few Days" is sandwiched between a visit to his mother's house and her death. But this long shadow hangs over most of his poems. The ending of an ordinary day is also a small death.

A Few Days: both what we're allotted in life and what's left to his mother as the poem begins.

> There's truth in the old saw. I
> have always been
> more interested in truth than in imagination: I
> wonder if that's
> true?
>
>   *
>
> And so I won't be
> there to see my Maney
> enearthed beside
> my stepfather:
> once when I was
> home a while ago
> I said I realized
> that in his way he
> loved me.

Schuyler will phrase a typical automatic response, "in his way he/loved me," which is no more than a reflex (we're always willing to dupe ourselves), and then show the process by which the truth edges toward him, and he records it.

> loved me. "He did
> not," my mother said.
> "Burton hated you."

Schuyler's lyrics take place in such a linear, circum-scribed time, beginning and ending within the arc of a day, or morning, that it comes as a relief when he starts to write long poems and allows himself as it were to let out more line. In the short poems there's the sense that he can only write about what's right in front of him. He'll often begin with the whole and end with the detail. And he is rarely on the move, walking.

Schuyler's long poems, "Hymn to Life," "The Morning of the Poem" and "A Few Days" document a reversal of the by now classic romantic position. Anti-didactic, anti-epiphanic, anti-self-improvement, he defines things by their unimportance and resists psychologizing why one memory, one perception, is connected to another. Schuyler mistrusts monumentality. I think he would find wisdom enervating. There is nothing of the set-piece in his long poems, the argument is built into the scaffolding of the work. Wordsworth, Eliot, and Milosz structure their long poems to appear inevitable: the high points brook no substitutions. But different stories, different events, would not change the character of Schuyler's long poems. He uses what he knows to frame the poem, which will be a record of discoveries. The process of telling is what compels him.

James Schuyler's work gives me hope for a new poetry, post modernist, post-post modern, post-Freudian, *pre—*

> Things should get better as you
>   grow older, but that
> is not the way. The way is inscrutable and hard to
>   handle.
>   ("A Few Days")

"Sometimes it is said of a man who lives alone, 'He does not like society.' Often it is as though one were to say that a man did not like walking because he would not choose to walk at night in the forest of Bondy."
—Sebastian Roch Nicolas de Chamfort

"What but design of darkness to appall?—
If design should govern a thing so small."
—Robert Frost

The notebook (journal, daybook, diary) is a form where the writer denies himself artifice. (Not that anyone would sit down to write one from beginning to end.) The entries surprise us through the absence of contexts. Epigraphs and quotations in novels or works of literary criticism can have a similarly startling effect (as in Stendhal's epigraphs to each chapter of *The Red and the Black*).

Notebook jottings can be as arresting as great lines of poetry—because you are not prepared for vision to appear like an apparition amidst the flux of daily life. It is hard to read a diary sequentially, which is why, even at their best, the brilliance of these isolated fragments can lose their luster unless they are placed in a larger, if albeit plotless, narrative, such as *Walden* or the *Notebooks of Malte Laurids Brigge.*

We are drawn toward journals out of a craving for the authentic, for the uncensored word and thought. The lack of context throws each line into relief. Among living writers Canetti's journals, *The Human Province*, are a record of this quest: "He would like to start from scratch. Where's scratch?" Or more straightforwardly: "Literature as a profession is destructive, one should *fear* words more."

In his notebooks the writer is offguard—but not entirely—there is still the dread of setting down words—of imprecision—just enough to increase the pendulum of significant trivia and generalizations about life that often border on the absurd, the interchangeably true or false. And he will not revise.

A journal is filled with errors. It is a composite of slips of the tongue, stabs in the dark, proposals, possibilities— statements that in not quite making sense transcend sense. Statements of such lucidity that we would not believe them if they were uttered by a character in a novel or a play.

In their tone of disclosure Kafka's diaries have the craft and cunning, if not the final form, of a work of art.

> October 30, 1921. Feeling of complete helplessness. What is it that binds you more intimately to these impenetrable, talking, eye-blinking bodies than to any other thing, the penholder in your hand, for example? Because you belong to the same species? But you don't belong to the same species, that's the very reason you raised the question. The impenetrable outline of human bodies is horrible. The wonder, the riddle of my not having perished already, of the silent power guiding me. It forces one to this absurdity: 'left to my resources, I should have long ago been lost.' My own resources.

That aside, in amazement at its own utterance—the phrase turned back on the writer who is alert to the void that opens when utterance becomes echo. Kafka is suspicious of fatuity. He is surprised and taken aback by his own utterances, at how far they stray from his intentions and gather other resonances. Words betray him. My *own resources*. The man, thrown back on himself again, refers to his own resources as if they were tangible. His insight betrays him, reminds him that the phrase is falsely consoling, for it is these resources that have fueled the feeling of self as other that Kafka embodies and is master of. He cannot resist following an image through, as though the beginning of a given utterance were fated to lead inevitably to an inward recognition.

> March 23, 1915. Incapable of writing a line. The feeling of ease with which I sat in Chotek Park yesterday and on the Karlsplatz today with Strindberg's *By the Open Sea*. My feeling of ease in my room today. Hollow as a clamshell on the beach, ready to be pulverized by the tread of a foot.

Imagination as prophecy. If Kafka is often inappropriately talked about as the man who foresaw the concentration camps and the bureaucracies of today in such works as *The Penal Colony* and *The Castle*, we can see the root of this capacity to predict or foresee in the progression of thought and image in these diary entries, moving from or to a neutral point through to a terrifying lucidity. The body, the world-body, words. The human body and language are equally "horrible," impenetrable. There is something comical in so studied a self-perception. To Kafka, the danger lay in thinking.

Thinking, like dreaming, could only distort the consolations of habit. Thought becomes action. The mind as ruined city. But instead of Troy or Rome, we have the mind contemplating the "impenetrable outline of bodies"—a portable tragedy if there ever was one. For Kafka the crisis begins only with thought: one reason why "K," who lays no claim to innocence, is such an innocent, perpetually astonished at what is happening to him.

Kafka, as he represents himself in his diaries, is already transformed, already the "K" of the novels. He never equates the words he writes with an intention independent of their expression. There was no private or public voice for him—only the voice that conveyed his vision.

The glimpses we get into the mystery of life, with no before or after—this is what allies lyric poetry, the aphorism, and the journal. Something we do not quite grasp latches onto our memory. It is when the image in the mind crosses with the image in the world. "The catastrophe of being alone," Peter Handke writes in *The Weight of the World*, "made acute by a missing button on the child's coat." In the journal, the writer is not trying to match Flaubert's desire for bears to dance on the "cracked kettle of language"; he's laying down a kind of graph of his imagination.

What Kafka does with "resources" and "ease" is not far removed from the skillful and elaborate conceit Hart Crane develops to open *The Bridge*, a series of resemblances that fade into the mind of an external world which exists only as long as he wills it to—the bridge, the seagull, the river—a world framed. It is an effort of will and intelligence to keep the image of the seagull before us, "Shedding white rings of tumult," ascend-

ing, "building high," then, remaining itself as it becomes other, matter turning into spirit, "with invio-
late curve," then disappearing at the edge of space and
taking with it all ease, returning the poem to a revery
on whiteness, forsaking "our eyes," and entering into
the mind of the dreamer at his office desk in front of
the page, "as apparitional as sails that cross/some page
of figures to be filed away"; falling into the body, "Till
elevators drop us from our day . . ./I think . . ."

It would be a mistake to deal with any journal as
truth, given our capacity for self-dramatization (for which
we may need no audience other than ourselves). Tolstoy is never more endearing, more human, than when,
in his diaries, he lists his trangressions, repents, promises
to remedy his ways, and as an afterthought can't help
saying that in spite of his failure to live up to high
moral standard he's still a better man than anyone he
knows. And, in the next day's entry, he "falls" again,
succumbs to lust—distracted by the rustling of the
chambermaid's skirts!

And—life imitates art. The notebook takes on an
internal form engendered by the life it is describing,
whether or not anything is said, for nowhere is the
hiatus between entries more telling. It is often easier
to believe the voice in these various journals than the
more willed voices of the author's "finished" works.
Witness Hopkins on April 8, 1873: "The ashtree growing
in the corner of the garden was felled. It was lopped
first; I heard the sound and looking out and seeing it
maimed there came at that moment a great pang and I
wished to die and not to see the inscapes of the world
destroyed any more . . ."

The journal offers a way of saying what you mean,
not what you think you mean. Not the kind of expla-

nations second thinking and hindsight offer. It can reflect a burst of sympathy or contempt when you notice that X's manner of walking lightly or heavily, slouching or standing very straight, telegraphs how he feels about himself, how he stands—or slouches—in relation to *things*. (Which are real because they have gravity.) Journals have this in common with slips of the tongue, which accounts in part for their eeriness. In Chekhov's notebook the bare bones of his perceptions were so true, so brutal, he needed a body, his humanity, for his reflections to mirror his vision accurately. If pure perception, removed from any moral boundary, were enough, he wouldn't have had to write his stories. He could have been an imagist.

A poet is interested in what he can quarry for poetry (what he can say "at a slant" by not "saying," what glimpses into the other world it is possible to reveal without a story).

Here is Thoreau, writing in his *Journal*, on February 18, 1852:

> I have a commonplace-book for facts and another for poetry, but I find it difficult always to preserve the vague distinction which I had in my mind, for the most interesting and beautiful facts are so much the more poetry and that is their success. They are *translated* from earth to heaven. I see that if my facts were sufficiently vital and significant—perhaps transmuted more into the substance of the human mind—I should need but one book of poetry to contain them all.

Eliot's astute definition of poetry corresponds to his method in both *The Waste Land* and the crucial passages, with their key images, in the *Four Quartets* (the moments in the rose garden, or in the arbor where the

rain beat, or the draughty church at smokefall): "Why,
for all of us, out of all that we have heard, seen, felt,
in a lifetime, do certain images recur, charged with
emotion, rather than others? The song of one bird,
the leap of one fish, at a particular place and time, the
scent of one flower, an old woman on a German mountain
path, six ruffians seen through an open window playing cards at night at a small French railway junction
where there was a water-mill: such memories may
have symbolic value, but of what we cannot tell, for
they come to represent the depths of feeling into which
we cannot peer. We might just as well ask why, when
we try to recall visually some period in the past, we
find in our memory just the few meager arbitrarily chosen
set of snapshots we do find there, the faded poor sou-
venirs of passionate moments." The stuff of notebooks.
The images in Eliot's list are all connected to nature,
wandering, movement, freedom, and youth. It is what
enchants us about *The Waste Land*.

> Summer surprised us, coming over the Starnbergesee
> With a shower of rain; we stopped in the colonnade,
> And went on in sunlight, into the Hofgarten,
> And drank coffee, and talked for an hour.

The notebook jotting can also take the form of a donnée.
The notebook consecrates the moment. The ubiquitious
Journal in early cubist paintings keys us in to the present,
the moment, the day. It doesn't matter so much what
happened on that day but that the day happened. The
day that particular doorknob appeared. And the date
marked on the newspaper marks the painting in time.
And it remains as constant as the other objects: bottle,
violin, glass, pipe, and inkstand. Even cubism only

remained new for as long as it could celebrate that. A notebook is an homage to surprise.

Try to imagine a moment of time as composed of matter, an inconceivably dense speck. Modern art and poetry take their cue from this moment. The idea that there is no objective reason for one moment to stand out over another defines the modern temperament.

No American poet recognized the potential of chance more than James Wright, who, albeit inspired by the example of Chinese poetry, grounded his poems in the precise event that inspired them. "A Message Hidden in An Empty Wine Bottle That I Threw Into A Gulley of Maple Trees One Night At An Indecent Hour," "From A Bus Window In Central Ohio, Just Before A Thunder Shower." If his syntax is linear and coherent, its origins are as mysterious as the leaps he makes, through parallelism, from section to section, for there is nothing extraordinary in the cirumstance that gave rise to them. To begin a poem he veers toward anecdote, or, as in "Miners," a newsworthy item: "the police *are probing tonight* for the bodies/ Of children in the black waters/Of the suburbs."

The most sincere journal may also be the saddest, especially those, like Camus' that are filled with resolutions, *shoulds*, and plans for work-to-be-done.

Read Owen.

Write the story of a contemporary cured of his heartbreaks solely by long contemplation of a landscape.

And on the facing page:

Prepare a book of political texts around Brasillach.

The danger in the form (as practiced) is portentous-ness. A book of days (lists) replete with generaliza-tions about life and death. A journal is not written for others, it is, as Rilke made clear with *Brigge*, for the other self, which the "I" may be in the process of creating: "So you [he is addressing Ibsen] began that unprecedented act of nature in your work, which, more and more impatiently, desperately, sought equivalents in the visible world for what you had seen inside."

There is something else which the notebook cannot escape: truth. And this impulse may extend into the literary work. The writer's own will to form works against the so-called random patterning of the note-book. Thoreau may have lied about the details of his life but we believe the voice in *Walden*, always verg-ing on the parable, who tells us, to greater purpose than the facts, that "I long ago lost a hound, a bay horse, and a turtle dove, and am still on their trail." Truth, in that sense, has to do with the feeling more than fact. Thoreau was a liar who told the truth. He made his private disclosure universal. The unstated axiom of the journal is this: The more deeply per-sonal, the more universal. This has nothing to do with the "I" in a poem or a story who is accountable to a place. This is the inner voice, the real self, void of distractions. The one we want to hear and may not be able to see. And distractions, in our culture, can take the most devious forms.

> I heard the dog barking outside in the evening; I am
> able to listen! (Happiness)
>   (Peter Handke, *The Weight of the World*)

I have often noted at an exhibition that a viewer will overlook an artist's grander conceptions and fix on the drawings. Or prefer the sketches to the finished work, as if the black and white and the diminutive allowed viewers to use their own imaginations more. I sometimes wonder if there isn't a human desire for incompleteness, which is reflected in the predilection for the small, the short, the fragment.

I want to talk about the genesis of "On Location."

*

This is as much a partial approach as it is a mis-reading.

*

I work from nature. The models for the woman and the child in the poem are my wife and son (then one-and-a-half), "in reality." The cliffs are part of Maine's metaphysical landscape where surf pounds black granite slabs.

*

The imagination wants to fix a visual sense of the world, of a necessarily eternal present, of the paradox of living in time, and of seeing things always as they will be only in that instant. But a poem needs a sustaining insight to corroborate perception and image.

*

"On Location" comes out of my obsession with the visible via the visual, the whole question of surfaces, the notion of what a "camera eye" can reveal. The equation of seeing and being. I have used this quote from Merleau-Ponty as an epigraph for the section of *The Nowhere Steps* in which the poem appears:

"We must reject that prejudice which makes 'inner realities' out of love, hate, or anger, leaving them accessible to one single witness: the person who feels them. Anger, shame, hate, and love are not psychic facts hidden at the bottom of another's consciousness: they are types of behavior or styles of conduct which are visible from the outside. They exist *on* this face or *in* those gestures, not hidden behind them" (Merleau-Ponty, "The Film and the New Psychology").

*

The woman draws her knees into her chest,
her hair all over her face.
(OL, 3)

*

How can we know what someone is going through if their gestures forbid us to read them? How do we know when someone is playing a role and when they are what they appear to be? The brilliance and limitation of cinema lies in its close-up of the human face.

*

There is a splendid moment in the film *The Middle of the World*, by Alain Tanner and John Berger, in which they crosscut images of the snow falling on a muddy field somewhere in "a neutral zone" (Switzerland) with the "drama" of their local heroes—a fed-up waitress whose inner life we know only through how she relates to objects, and yet who is imbued with the grace of a woman in a Vermeer painting, and a dissatisifed young businessman who falls briefly in love with her until "reason" teases him out of it—so that when Phillipe Leotard eats some snow after they tumble down a slope together it is a joyous action: he takes a bite out of the universe!—before he stiffens and retreats into local politics.

Can film offer anything toward a poetics of the future, when most cinematic techniques (montage, narrative, the silent images of fields and skylines) derive from poetry and the novel? The late French critic André Bazin came up with the term "deep (or depth) focus" to describe certain films of the late thirties by Renoir and Wyler which had broken away from the by then neutralized techniques of montage and close-up. The reaction shot overdetermines the viewer's response. It does the thinking for you. In deep focus the camera's held at a middle distance. The viewer's gaze is not fixed on the protagonists: it places them within a context where other people and objects have equal space, equal time. The world keeps on trailing off into more world. It suggests that the other characters have a story too, and that the landscape exists before and after the characters enter and exit. It shows the boundaries of their world. It de-centralizes. It gives the camera the chance to show the unbroken continuum of reality. Deep focus accomplishes effortlessly and without pretension what many writers and artists struggle to do to be "postmodern."

It's possible for a poem to attain something like deep focus. Foreground and background can come forward and recede with each reading. The objects of attention can float from a woman's barrette to the cleft in a cliff. And the poem can reawaken us to the fact that, as John Cage says, the sounds of the world are taking place all the time.

"Depth of focus," Bazin claimed, "reintroduced ambiguity into the structure of the image." He sees Jean Renoir as an innovator who forced himself to look back beyond the resources of montage to uncover "the secret of a film form that would permit everything to be said without chopping the world up into little fragments, that would reveal the hidden meanings in people and things without disturbing the unity natural to them."

There is much that poetry can quarry from Pinter's screenplay of *Remembrance of Things Past* for the way it condenses the novel to its spots of time, non-linear reverberating causal links made visible.

> 15. In the library, MARCEL, a glass by his side, wipes his lips with a stiff napkin, which crackles.
> 16. Venice. Window in a palazzo. Silent.
> 17. In the drawing room, a group of very old women, talking.
> 18. Water pipes in the library.
> The shrill noise of water running through the pipes.
> 19. Silent countryside from the railway carriage.

*

Eisenstein derived montage from Dickens. Think of how differently cinema might have developed if it had evolved from Flaubert.

*

Poetry is as relentlessly inward as cinema is outward. In poems we may *only* know what someone is feeling and thinking; in cinema this knowledge eludes us.

*

No matter what I say here, when I started to write the poem, I had nothing in mind so much as certain sounds, a rhythm, and the desire to transmit what I was hearing, make it audible to others. The music that the mind construes is the only intelligible sign of the poem's existence.

*

Moving pictures enable us to visualize time, albeit at twenty four frames a second.

A poet's choice of form is a stance in relation to time.

Narrative is comforting, reaffirming, social. It unfolds in time like music. Lyric cuts a hole through time. Though it takes its impulse from song, lyric is closer to painting in the way it arrests time. We don't need time to grasp Vaughn's line: "I saw eternity the other night."

*

One formal rule I made for myself in "On Location" was to stay outside, on the surface.

I always think of form, à la Brecht, as antithetical. Narrate the terrible comprehensibly.

The dialectics of composition: cool treatment of a hot subject. The formal equivalent of an anti-mask.

*

Certain events are *as if*; certain events are absolute. Nearly everyone confuses them.

*

There is a desire to proceed like a detective—hanging on the "as if," as if a connection could be made, a whole sensed in the ruin of instants, moments robbed of continuity—to reclaim from the world's weight what is too often lost.

*

We are impelled to write by our knowledge that mo-

ments will never recur, that the sprig of green on the
(nearly) bare tree on the avenue will not be there long—

I say this in another way in a recent poem, "Conversation: December, The Night City."

> Nothing happens the same way twice.
> And yet we court repetition.
> And the milky sky above the city blurs what lies
> above this sky.
>
> *
>
> Vast spray of buildings.
>
> Every kind of light but starlight.
>
> *

All we can know of the world is what exists in the
present moment, the anxious instant, but we deny this
at most every moment of our lives. The only way out
of theory is to return to non-linear, non-syllogistic, double-
brained thinking. Intuition leading logic by the hand.
Being apprehensive about the future is a form of magical
thinking, a way of making it exist. And so we are
released into chaos, into chopped up time, freed from
the burden of repetition. Detours occupy the center.

> Did the camera know when it followed her to the
>   cliff's edge
> what would happen? That she would
>
> leap? The director never tells the actors what will
>   happen
> in advance. The cliff rises sheer above the gray-black
>
> waters. Night advances as a filter covers the lens.
> "Let's do it again, and this time, don't look

like you know what you're going to do."
She walks briskly out to the cliff, like someone

who wanted to shake memories out of her body,
(OL, 1)

*

A friend read an early draft of "On Location" and asked
me if I had gotten the idea from Robert Stone's *Children of Light*, which hadn't yet been published when
the poem was conceived. That book hinges around
filming Kate Chopin's *The Awakening*, which I have not
read.

*

In "On Location" I try to take an event, a portion of
an action, and make that stand as an emblem for a
life. I wanted the poem to have its own language, a
kind of cross between a screenplay (direct, unmediated
description) and a lyrical meditation. To marry the
two forms, I used unrhymed couplets derived from
the ghazal to undercut any potential narrative implication, what Handke calls "the gentle emphasis and
appeasing flow of narrative." Couplets seemed appropriate as a way of continually introducing a "story"
I did not plan to tell, or retell. The couplets put the
right amount of white space between dissimilar objects. They form a temporary resolution of the irresolvable.

*

All treatment of subject in poetry is metaphorical.

*

The story is a known quantity. "All these stories are
the same," attests Michael Palmer (echoing Robert Graves'
famous line in "To Juan at the Winter Solstice"?): "There

is only one story—//but not really—."

*

The crew, glimpsed through its brief dialogue, is clearly on location.

"It drags. It's too meditative."

"It needs a violent death."
(OL, 2)

Clichés are the tautologies of the vernacular.

*

The scenes for the unnamed movie alternate with scenes the actress seems to observe. She, too, is viewer, glancing out, as if through a lens,

a chewed hole in the boarded window toward a spot

on the rocks where a woman hands a child a banana, which he squinches in his fist and grins.
(OL, 2)

It is possible that what she sees is going on inside her head as she walks and reflects her longing.

*

The sequence reflects a series of possibilities: the actress feels some identification with the character she plays. Yet she is immobile, condemned to a fixed posture, curious melancholy, where the woman she plays is expressive. Her expression of grief is effortless. Perhaps the contrast between the naturalness of the woman and the child and the actress come from their different attitudes toward what it means to be seen. The actress anticipates that someone, some eye, is watching her.

How much of what she thinks can that observing eye discern from what is shown, from what it sees played out on the visual plane?

*

Poetry has difficulty evoking relations between men and women. Not the feeling of one sex about the other, only relations between them. We are tired of a poetry solely of the wronged party, and interested in how reality provokes a circumstance. Rooms and cliffs serve a similar role: they frame our mortal purposes.

*

I do think that the hypothetical camera eye catches the gist of the actress's ambivalence. Is the woman she sees through the "chewed hole in the boarded window" also her offscreen self? I attempt to open up these questions with the poem, not round them out.

*

I had the eerie experience recently of glancing at an article about Jane Fonda in *Vanity Fair* and noting that Ron Rosenbaum used much the same language to describe Fonda's life "on the edge" and the parts she plays as I used to describe the imaginary actress in "On Location." "She's been known to drive herself to the edge," he writes "and over, before."

> She walks briskly out to the cliff, like someone//

> who wanted to shake memories out of her body.
> (OL, 1)

> She's no longer on the lawn that's been carved out of

the wilds.
The wilderness she longs for drives her over the
    edge.
                    (OL, 4)

                    *

For the purposes of the script, if not for the poem, she
disappears at the end, and the camera continues to
shoot the landscape without her.

    Thrum of lobster boats, hiss of tide over shells,
    "sounds human and inhuman...,"

    the faint churring of an engine,
    and boats that,(—it is written in the script—)

    like "reminders of the human heart,"
    slip in and out of sight.
                    (OL, 4)

The poem plies certain clichés that lie close to truths.
Thus the use of brackets, ellipses, quotation marks, parentheses.

                    *

"On Location" is a study in irony. Everything is sus-
pect, private lives, the effect of observation on behavior. Doesn't the intention to create meaning, to say
this and not say that, force us into postures? We see
people acting, we see them without interiority, this is
both challenge and tragedy: we "gotta use words," as
Eliot's Sweeney says, and words betray us.

                    *

Some years ago, as a friend and I trudged across Central Park through the February slush, I remarked that
from where we stood at dusk with the lights begin-

ning to go on all around us the city looked like Venice—
a stage-set. He replied: "The whole world is a stage-
set."

*

On this level, "On Location" can be read as a series of
metaphors for how the real and the possible, the banal
and the magical, interpenetrate life and poetry.

*

Poetry is on location. It does not describe events, only
the seismic reverberation at the edges.

*

There are analogies to this poetic process in the sci-
ences. In chaos theory "Faults and fractures so dominate the structure of the earth's surface that they become the key to any good description, more important
on balance than the material they run through" (James
Gleick, *Chaos*). Chaos gives precedence to variables.

*

An incident or situation sets off an unremembered memory
trace that simultaneously seeks a form. The music is
in the mind and it precedes the poem and follows in
its wake. Then comes the attempt to subdue the material and the pattern that we recognize as ours emerges.
The pattern is a mystery. Why do we approach the
poem the way we do: why does one cleave to the left
hand margin (choosing, decisively, upper or lower case);
why does another spread words across the "open field"
of the page?

*

Are the actions in the poem central or peripheral? Is
the color of the sky a real and vivid image of our moods?
Does the heron redeem anything?

a blue heron, motionless mirage,
stands in the mud flats when the tide is out

and which, upon being sighted, disappears,
without a wingbeat, without a sign.
(OL, 4)

The heron disappears the moment it is seen.

*

I question epiphany: I believe in the radiant instant.

*

The landcape in "On Location" provides a romantic setting which is already charged with portents, already a cliché. These cliffs and beaches preceded the poem and the prospective movie. The symbolism of landscape, of a landscape, is what we bring to it. In "On Location" what interests me most is how the ultra-mundane images of the woman and the child contrast with the timeless, elemental scene.

*

I like the idea of positioning people at the edges of things. I use urban problems against the background of the pastoral to heighten the conflicts, make them stand out in relief. So many of the problems in an urban setting have to do with others. The pastoral gives us a chance to reckon our fate against eternity.

*

This is, at bottom, the poem's crisis:

(Why is it only the dark that grows?)
(OL, 4)

1

For Pound "to break the pentameter . . . was the first heave" and the same was true for Ginsberg, Merwin, most of the Black Mountain poets, and many of the generation of American poets born in 1926 and '27. To escape the anxiety that comes from a poets' taking a larger role in the community, the "return to form" has occupied itself almost exclusively with verse technique, with what can be measured against content. This is neutral ground. I remember Auden telling me how I missed a beat in the villanelle Paul Nemser and I wrote for his seminar, and that's all he concerned himself with. (We were the only students to do his assignment. Metrical poetry was out of fashion then.) It wasn't a debatable point, and that's why external form is so attractive now: you resurrect "standards" without any reference to moral or ethical imperatives. I always remember that it was Wittgenstein who in the *Tractatus* insisted on the necessary unity between ethics and aesthetics: Ethics and aesthetics are one. Wittgenstein, Trakl's anonymous patron, who was willing to back him while claiming not to "understand" (whatever that means) his work. . . . There is no poetry without form. Some poets imaginations thrive on the specific boundaries of rhyme and meter. I do think that free verse opened up possibilities for language that have only begun to be explored, much less exhausted, and that it is retrograde to write primarily in fixed forms. These "forms," from the regular use of rhyme and meter to the production of pantoums and sestinas and villanelles, are to my mind a simplification, and an escape from deeper formal issues.

2

The risk involved in writing free verse carries a lot of responsibility and anxiety. Any laxness on the part of the poet and it becomes its dreaded counterpart, prose. It is understandable that, in their anxiety that poetry should not be prose, and that poetry should be easily separable from prose, that some poets would have us abandon free verse to clear up the boundary. Good prose can be very good. Or is it poetry?

Pound's obsession with that which was carved in stone. The Acmeist obsession with the same. "Romance of the precise." Movements bearing false analogies to give its practitioners footholds in something they imagined to be real.

Suspicion of free verse among its practitioners. Williams's insistent search for definitions, as though the need for breathing room in the poem needed to be given greater credibility.

From Mandelstam's essay, "The Morning of Acmeism": "What sort of idiot would agree to build if he did not believe in the reality of his material, the resistance of which he must overcome?... We do not fly: we ascend only such towers as we ourselves are able to build."

Mandelstam wrote only one poem in free verse, "The Ode to the Horseshoe," and it is a kind of *ars poetica*.

> Where to begin?
> Everything cracks and shakes.
> The air trembles with similes.
> No one word is better than any other,
> the earth moans with metaphor
> . . .
>
> Human lips,
>   that have nothing more to say,
> keep the shape of the last word uttered,
> and the hand keeps feeling the weight
> even though the jug
>   splashed itself half empty
>   while being
>   carried home.
>
> What I'm saying now isn't said by me,
> it's dug up out of the ground like grains of petrified
>   wheat.
>   (Translated by Clarence Brown)

His "Conversation About Dante" is a sourcebook for the poetry of the future, and though it is tempting to quote from endlessly I will limit myself to one passage. "Let us imagine a monument of granite or marble the symbolic function of which is not to represent a horse or a rider but to disclose the inner structure of the very marble or granite itself. In other words, imagine a monument of granite which has been erected in honor of granite and as though for the revelation of its idea. You will then receive a rather clear notion of how form and content are related in Dante."

*

Joyce and Proust are always more "poetic," in the old sense, than Williams and Pound. Because what is poetic has nothing to do with poetry as such anymore but belongs equally and indifferently to poetry and prose.

Emerson in "The Poet": "We need not metres but a metre-making argument." (What more is there to say?)

Basil Bunting's *Briggflats* seems to me to be a good example of how free verse can be seen as an advance over the strictly metrical. "A mason times his mallet/ to a lark's twitter/listening while the marble rests," rhythm drawing its sound from the world's body.

> The solemn mallet says:
> In the grave's slot
> he lies. We rot.
> . . .
>
> Brief words are hard to find,
> shapes to carve and discard:
> . . .
>
> It is easier to die than to remember.
> Name and date
> split in soft slate
> a few months obliterate.
> . . .
>
> Starlight quivers. I had day enough.
> For love uninterrupted night.

Free verse—with rhyme? The rhymes have been dictated by the materials, the "solemn mallet"(s) repetitions. "Uninterrupted" equals an inconceivable time of endless duration. A wordless word.

3

Other examples: Roethke's "The Meadow Mouse," "Now
he's eaten his three kinds of cheese and drunk from
his bottle-cap watering-trough—"and "The Geranium."
His identification with "all things innocent, hapless,
forsaken," gives the rhythm a gravity and finality that
the subject would otherwise belie. And, in many of
his other poems, an Elizabethan bittersweet toughness,
a range and complexity of tones and sonorities. Take
this passage in "Praise to the End":

> Now the water's low. The weeds exceed me.
> It's necessary, among the flies and bananas, to keep a
>   constant vigil,
> For the attacks of false humility take sudden turns for
>   the worse.
> Lacking the candor of dogs, I kiss the departing air;
> I'm untrue to my own excesses.

But Roethke was also later trapped within his own concept
of what constituted poetic intensity. There is, in general, a reluctance to look at the implications of the line
that follows the oft quoted "Praise to the end!" in *The
Prelude*: "Thanks likewise to the means!"

*

Williams' "The Drunk and the Sailor" is another poem
rooted in a powerful recognition about the self through
an encounter with another—and another—heretofore
buried, invisible part of the self. The psychological
connection between the imagined scene and the pain
alongside it imbues the language with a mysterious
power. I want to quote the Williams poem in full because it is less well known than the others and, though
it is quite memorable its virtues are less obvious.

THE DRUNK AND THE SAILOR

The petty fury
  that disrupts my life—
      at the striking of a wrong key
as if it had been
  a woman lost
or a fortune . .
  The man was obviously drunk,
      Christopher Marlowe
could have been no drunker
  when he got himself
      stuck through the eye
with a poniard.
  The bus station was crowded.
The man
  heavy-set
      about my own age
seventy
  was talking privately
      with a sailor.
He had an ugly jaw on him.
  Suddenly
      sitting there on the bench
too drunk to stand
  he began menacingly
      his screaming.
The young sailor
  who could have flattened him
      at one blow
kept merely looking at him.
  The nerve-tingling screeches
      that sprang
sforzando
  from that stubble beard
      would have distinguished
an operatic tenor.

But me—
the shock of it—
my heart leaped in my chest
so that I saw red
wanted
to strangle the guy
The fury of love
is no less.

Williams whole psychic life is embodied here, where
the doppelgänger motif takes place in the light of day:
he sees his past and present self reflected both in the
young sailor and in the old man, "about my own age/
seventy," he wants to strangle. The drama of the poem
is in how it builds toward that recognition. It's difficult to imagine a more potent "flat" line than "The
bus station was crowded." It arrests the action and
functions like a stage direction to open up the way for
the power of "he began menacingly/his screaming,"
which is the way to say it—when there's something
wrong but you don't know what—yet.

4

Where does free verse take its cue? One place is in
Hotspur's opening jag in *Henry IV*. The actions he
describes and the emotions behind them seem to invoke the rhythm of the language that ensues:

But I remember, when the fight was done,
When I was dry with rage and extreme toil,
Breathless and faint, leaning upon my sword,
Came there a certain lord, neat, and trimly dress'd,
Fresh as a bridegroom; and his chin new reap'd
Show'd like a stubble-land at harvest home;
He was perfumed like a milliner;
And twixt his finger and his thumb he held

A pouncet box, which ever and anon
He gave his nose and took 't away again;
Who therewith angry, when it next came there,
Took it in snuff; and still he smiled and talk'd,
And as the soldiers bore dead bodies by,
He called them untaught knaves, unmannerly,
To bring a slovenly unhandsome corse
Betwixt the wind and his nobility.

Hotspur has his own language, yet *Hotspur does not exist*. The matter at hand to be conveyed generates the words, the magnificent yet immediate piling up of qualifiers and clauses, each of which exists due to an emotional pressure, a specific agitation, the matter, the material, at hand. And later in the play this man of action says, like an anti-poet, to refute the moonstruck magician Glendower (the scene between these two is one of the high points of debate about poetics), in words that are almost prophetic of the manifestoes to come:

I had rather be a kitten and cry mew
Than one of these same metre ballad-mongers.

5

After Shakespeare, Wordsworth is the precursor of free verse in getting poetry to expand its capacity to integrate materials. The most memorable passages in *The Prelude* are also concerned with *movement*: skating, boating, climbing Snowden. Free verse, once it broke clear of imagist imperatives, a limitation become a distraction, concerned itself with movement: And then went down to ships, set keel to anchor. There was always information being conveyed, as if in synchronous concurrence with Husserl's idea that consciousness is always consciousness of something.

6

Free verse, of course, is a misnomer. "No verse is free ..."

Free verse: a poetry in which, to put it crudely, something is happening. To break away from nostalgia.

Free verse, by now, is a classical mode. The inscriptions on cave walls, the psalms.

One cannot account for the power of free verse without recourse to the novel. Cross fertilization and interplay of forms. Prose began to take over the domain of the long poem and the epic.

Pound's *Mauberley* speaks for this: "His true Penelope was Flaubert . . ."

Free verse attempts to set the prose of the world to music.

It is not far from "the language of men" to free verse. And each step forward is an attempt to integrate and quarry more material from the real. Impurities boost the paradigm.

But much modern poetry follows in the footsteps of the novel: Pound and Eliot take the milieu and an attitude toward subject matter of their early work from James; Akhmatova, Mandelstam, and Pasternak, from Tolstoy. It has to do with how to embody the commonplace, how to employ detail. (This, more than "family matters," exemplifies Robert Lowell's project and lasting influence, and the sudden surge of interest in Elizabeth Bishop.)

"But what do you mean by detail?"

The metonymic imagination: With Stevens and Pasternak it is the weather, the season, thistles or the trees at a meeting that speak, as in *The Highest Sickness*:

> Poverty stricken February
> groaned, coughed blood,
> and tiptoed off to whisper
> into the ears of boxcars
> about this and that,
> railroad ties and tracks,
> the thaw, and babbled on, of troops
> foot-slogging home from the front.

7

The world, Bronowski insisted, following Leakey, cannot be grasped by meditation. The new formalism arose just after the so-called poetry of voice began to dominate the scene and is almost welcome as a corrective to that lax "I," as against eye-oriented, indulgent stuff. Poetry seeks tension and release from tension. Some of the people writing in form today are reacting to that poetry, which is at once formless and formulaic. What we lament in the "free verse" being written today is the absence of sound.

There's a danger of reductiveness in all schematic inquiry. (Even Bachelard can be reductive.)

Rhythm, rather than rhyme, is the goal of any poetry. And yet when Mayakovsky talks about rhyming in order to remember his own poems which he composed as he walked, who can quarrel with that? Many poets are stimulated by formal constraints. And it's a mistake to underestimate the purely ludic factor.

8

Oppen's comment on why Reznikoff was so slow to gain the recognition he deserved (the same being true of himself); that his poetry is *"merely* perfect and profound and infinitely moving" (my emphasis) and "that he is of little use to those who would teach or explicate a poem . . . The least of Rezi's one line poems says more—does more—than anything one can say about it."

> Once a toothless woman opened her door,
> chewing a slice of bacon that hung from her mouth
>   like a tongue.

> This is where I walked night after night;
> this is where I walked away many years.

In passages such as this poetry has made a giant step forward, and its relation to prose is not a thing to be despised.

9

Reading Bronk's *Careless Love*. Something the poems leave unsaid moves me: "a face/a leaf, a certain light which prompts us to see,/as in a mirror's *blank* . . ." A reluctant eloquence. Being able to breathe in the interstices of what is left unsaid. In such dislocations as "The stove is out" in "Worlds and Changes" which recapitulates a life's experience in its context. Maybe the point is that the lyrical statement can never be taken literally. What is free about this verse?

Title of the book that brought Oppen back to poetry after a silence of twenty five years, *The Materials*.

The pressure should be everywhere and invisible.

The question of syntax.

10

How one takes refuge in form as in a harbor, "hugging the shore," to borrow Updike's phrase that is as applicable in terms of a distinction between poetry and verse as it is in terms of criticism versus fiction. Diminished risks.

Leopardi: "For men are willing to suffer almost anything from each other or from heaven itself, so long as *true words* to not touch them."

But when anxiety surrounds us as the night used to, why not pull the blanket up over our heads, and return to form?

Leopardi: "Men are miserable by necessity, yet determined to think themselves miserable by accident."

Is this the same as the return to the figure and the image in painting? Or the swing back toward straight narrative in film after the discontinuous (non-narrative) work of Antonioni, Resnais, Godard, Bergman, Altman and others?

There is no point in "returning to form" because there is no external form to return to, no fixed neutral element waiting to be reactivated by the well-intentioned poet.

I hate the separation of poets into formal camps. Poetry transcends attitudes and predilections, even sensibilities. The best poets never fit into any camp.

The animus we sense in the air transcends the peccadilloes of individuals. Mandelstam gives substance to this in "Some Notes on Poetry," an essay/review of Pasternak's *My Sister—Life*: "In poetry, war is always being waged. It is only in periods of social imbecility that there is peace or a peace treaty is concluded. Like generals, the bearers of word roots take up arms against each other. Word roots battle in the darkness, depleting each other's food supplies and the juices of the earth."

11

Larkins's *Required Writings*. With what shrewdness and drollery does he toss off some outrageous maxims. One statement in particular activated my interest and ire, "Writing poetry is playing off the natural rhythms and word-order of speech *against the artificialities of rhyme and meter*," (my emphases) as though *that* were all there were to the matter. The answer lies in our senses, not in our aesthetics. A poet is not a phenomenologist, even if he may equate seeing with being. And if he doesn't have a music in his head, and an idea of what he wants to do that is higher than the realm of restrictions that would constrain him, why would he bother?

And yet it is only the context creating second part of Larkin's sentence I disagree with. Are rhyme and meter the *only* "artificialities," objective, intractable, against which a poet can play off the natural rhythms and word-order of speech? Or is not this rhyme and meter that which is embedded in the tradition, as a pressure that is everywhere and invisible as basic structures as well as in the poem being made.

*

John Hollander speaks to the idea of false distinctions in the current *Paris Review*: "I find free verse very, very difficult to write; in the past, when I've written free verse, I've felt the constraints some people must feel trying to write couplets. I don't know why some people have an ideology about form—"open," "closed," whatever." "Each poet evolves individually."

12

Absence of trust in the unknown quantity, in the unmeasurable aspect of form. Robert Frost's characteristically witty and vicious line about free verse being like playing "tennis without the net." My rejoinder to that is that it's much more difficult to have to imagine the boundaries.

Playing Kadima ("smash ball") on the dock while waiting for the ferry on Swan's Island, an island on the Maine coast, I thought, this is harder than tennis because there is no net. The free verse poem is played off against the genre and tradition, familiar lines, touchstones. The form responds to the poet's sense of what is possible. Frost was an innovative poet; his use of speech rhythms

and casual diction was radical. Frost is subtle where
Hardy is bold, and there was enough in these tensions
and contradictions for him to explore throughout his
life. He was threatened by the idea of non-memorable
lines and he had every right to be. History may show
"The Death of the Hired Man" (and other of Frost's
dramatic poems) to be as innovative a poem as "Zone."
His lyrics ask to be memorized:

> I have been one acquainted with the night.
> I have walked out in rain—and back in rain.
> I have outwalked the furthest city light.

And yet we can memorize Apollinaire's poem too, which
rhymes in spite of its cubist construction, radical juxtapositions, and unpunctuated lines,

> Et tu observes au lieu d'écrire ton conte en prose
> La cétoine qui dort dans le coeur de la rose

and even in Samuel Beckett's translation:

> And you observe instead of writing your story in
>   prose
> The chafer asleep in the heart of the rose

Death is what gnaws at the core of the poet's work.

*

But does a poem like Williams' "The Desert Music"
ask to be memorized? When I think of it I see it on
the page and remember only words like *Juarez, sequins,
flange, girder*.

Now the music volleys through as in
a lonely moment I hear it. Now it is all
about me. The dance! The verb detaches itself
seeking to become articulate.

13

The straight genres have been exhausted, and we need
a radical yet revisionary spirit to "make it *live*" (rather
than "new").

11/27—12/5, 1985

Boris Pasternak, Marina Tsvetayeva, and Rainer Maria Rilke
LETTERS: Summer 1926, edited by Yevgeny Pasternak,
Yelena Pasternak, and Konstantin M. Azadovsky and
translated by Margaret Wettlin and Walter Arndt.

As the title conveys, this book is the correspondence
between Pasternak, Tsvetayeva, and Rilke, in the summer of 1926. Pasternak and Tsvetayeva are in mid-
career; Rilke is dying, but doesn't know it.

Since the revolution Russian poetry has been under
pressure to contain a positive social message as well
as be "comprehensible" (in quotes because true art never
reveals its meaning so easily). There is nothing "occa-
sional" here. Even the literary gossip is passionate
gossip. For the two Russian poets especially, a lot was
at stake: only in these letters could Pasternak and Tsvetayeva
say what they had to say to each other. For them the
letter was a life or death matter. In Pasternak's words:
"I fear death only because it is I who will die, without
having had the chance to be everyone else. But sometimes when I am writing to you or reading what you
have written, I am free of this clattering, jostling threat."

These letters are literature. All three poets are as
eloquent here as they are in any of their other works.
The writing is at all times bold, consistent with their
other work: same high tone, even the same phrases. I
was not surprised to read that Tsvetayeva drafted them

in a notebook before writing them. Correspondence used to be a literary form. (Correspondence = correspondences.) The death of correspondence may lead to a dearth of correspondences, the loss of one of the primary ways that language is transformed into an alternate reality. And I would argue that the decline of this type of correspondence has given birth to poetry—verse really—that is less intense. My urge to write about the book arises from my conviction that this passionate relationship in letters—and to letters—carries important lessons for our generation. Today we have a growing severance between public and private selves. Passion and immediacy fall to the side when the "poem" becomes a thing apart from the rhythm of life and, existing then in a sealed off aesthetic realm, it is often too private and not private enough.

Rilke stands at the center of the book like the ghost of Hamlet's father: an awesome presence though his appearances are scarce. Rilke has just completed the *Duino Elegies* and the *Sonnets to Orpheus*. And he has answered the question of the *Elegies*, "Who if I cried would hear me among the angelic orders" in the *Sonnets* with his hymn to inwardness, the temple inside the ears of pure listening.

A conditional hazard for these three temperaments was that love remained distant, so filled was it with longing for the absolute. Or, in Rilke, transpersonal love: a springboard to independence, as in this passage from *Duino Elegies*:

> Is it not time that, in loving,
> we freed ourselves from the loved one, and,
>   quivering, endured,
> as the arrow endures the string, to become, in the
>   gathering out-leap,

something more than itself? For staying is nowhere.
(Spender/Leishman translation)

And Pasternak and Tsvetayeva are aware, though they
never mention it in so many words, that with Rilke's
death an era will end.   Rilke, for all of his aestheti-
cism, lived his life as an experiment in freedom.   He
registered a progress from matter to spirit, thingness
to no-thing, "when the wind full of infinite space/de-
vours our faces."   The longing for the absolute that
Rilke experienced will come to be seen as too precious
for the modern, post World War II, post revolution
sensibility throughout the Western world.   But when
Rilke is gone, Pasternak and Tsvetayeva will be left
and forced to negotiate boundaries.   Their lives will
become the very antithesis of his.   His death will swallow
up the solitude out of which he spoke.   A life without
compromise.   Rilke never felt he had to please anyone.   The Russian poets face an excruciating choice:
either they will have to please the powers that be in
order to stay alive and publish, or they will have to
fall silent, or at best insinuate their meaning through
tertiary literary activities, such as translation.

In fact, it seems as if this is the moment when Baudelaire's
forest of symbols is becoming internalized by these poets,
a forest of symbols whose codes could be transmitted
through dailiness. By 1926, it is only possible for Pasternak
and Tsvetayeva to tell the truth directly when artifice
is lowered.   And ordinary things were to be imbued
with value through the quality of detail, light (romance
of the precise), cadences.   Equivalences no longer had
to be drawn.   The moon could return to being the moon.
In these letters they reveal everything by speaking in
a certain exaggerated tone of voice because they trust

the addressee. Hyperbole takes on the weight of symbol.

But Pasternak and Tsvetayeva's shift should not be perceived as a decline. Being released from the weight of the symbol into the real is a form of transcendence where *things* could take on symbolic weight through the context in which they were placed. Tsvetayeva's "always stove, broom, money (none)" resonates much in the same way that Pasternak's "steppe, haystack, groan" does at the end of *My Sister—Life*.

> Another street. Another night. Another canopy of
>   tulle.
> Once again—steppe, haystack, groan
> now and forever.

At the same time, the book provides a study in contrasts in the way this shift is negotiated. Pasternak is in his uneven, awkward, hybrid, elliptical yet fascinating middle period after the purely lyrical success of *My Sister—Life* and *Themes and Variations*. He is writing or has just written *Lieutenant Schmidt, The Year 1905,* and the most complex and tortured of these poems, *The Highest Sickness.*

> Although, as before, the ceiling,
> installed to support a new cell,
> lugged the second story to the third
> and dragged the fifth to the sixth
> suggesting by this shift that everything
> was as it used to be—
> and anyway, it was all a forgery;
> and through the network of waterpipes
> rushed the hollow reverberation
> of a dark age; the stench

of laurel and soybean,
smoldering in the flames of newspapers
even more indigestible than these lines,
rises into air like a pillar
as though muttering to itself: Hold on, prompt me,
what did I want to eat?

Tormented by his conscience, he is trying to pay heed to the needs of "the age," and half failing, half succeeding, always stretching himself beyond what he'd done before, which is what gives his work of this period its odd, factual, fantastical quality. Pasternak is in crisis, personal and aesthetic; hounded by family responsiblities, his tone is often as oblique in these letters as it is in the poems. His poetry is caught between his old style and his style to be of *Second Birth*. But he knows what he is after.

Tsvetayeva writes with high confidence, which is as it should be since she is writing at the height of her power in poems like "Poem of the Mountain" and "Poem of the End" and "The Pied Piper" in the moments she snatched from her chores and taking care of her children. She envisions herself as always holding a broom. In one of her last letters to Rilke she writes: "What have I seen of life? Throughout my youth (from 1917 on)—black toil. Moscow? Prague? Paris? St.-Gilles? Same thing. Always stove, broom, money (none). Never any time. No woman among your acquaintances and friends lives like that, would be capable of living so. Not to sweep any more—of that is my kingdom of heaven."

And we have Pasternak, who takes a long time to say, almost always indirectly, what he means. And we have Tsvetayeva, who goes right for the target; not that she always knows her heart. And we have Rilke, who stands aloof, almost Olympian, while still remaining one of them. "You, poet, (he writes to Tsvetayeva) do you sense how you have overwhelmed me, you and your magnificent fellow reader; I'm writing like you and I descend like you the few steps down from the sentence into the mezzanine of parentheses, where the ceilings are so low and where it smells of roses past that never cease. Marina: how I have inhabited your letter."

Interesting, too, the subtext here: a drama between the lines of these letters lying in the fact that years before Pasternak never responded to a letter Rilke wrote him. (The two had met when Pasternak was a child at his father's house, and Pasternak remembers Rilke in the opening passage of *Safe Conduct*, which is dedicated to him—as someone "in a dark Tyrolese cape.") A resounding chord through the book is his guilt over this seemingly easy to solve matter. And then he ends his autobiography, *Safe Conduct*, begun shortly after the correspondence, with a letter to Rilke supposedly "explaining everything." "It was not easy for me to leave unacknowledged a gift as precious as your kind words. But I feared that, content with corresponding with you, I would never reach you in person. And I had to see you. Until that time came I would not write to you."

Rilke, writing to Pasternak's father, Leonid Pasternak, mentions that he has seen some of Boris' poems in Helene Iswolsky's French translation. Leonid reports Rilke's praise to Boris who in turn puts Rilke in touch with Tsvetayeva. Some of the interchanges between father and son are spicy, even bizarre, as when Leonid reproves Boris for referring to him, in a letter he is to forward to Rilke, by his initials, as "L.O." This gesture by the younger Pasternak is somehow charac-

teristic of his relationship to figures of authority in a
way that is difficult to pin down. Even his father can't
seem to do it though he tries:

> I cannot help drawing your attention to a certain
> faux pas you made in your letter to him (Rilke) which
> even an outsider would find offensive . . . I know
> you had nothing offensive in mind when you wrote,
> "In your letter to L.O. . ." . . . the point is that there
> is an implied "somebody-or-other" in that abbrevi-
> ated form (it looks even worse in German); if you
> do not feel it I cannot explain it, but it would have
> been simpler to say "to my father." It reminds me of
> some newspaper reporters who came to interview
> me once and began, "Begging your pardon, do you
> happen to be L.O?"

And so the letters sweep from family misunderstandings
to the most elevated forms of literary criticism. When
Pasternak and Tsvetayeva respond to one another's poems,
the criticism is at as high a level of understanding as I
have ever encountered. They each know exactly what
the other is attempting at every level and go right to
the nerve when they praise or point to trouble spots.
And this is the way it is with true poets, though the
public never sees it. Pasternak on Tsvetayeva's "The
Pied Piper":

> The rhythm itself seems to be made not out of words
> but of rats, and not of word stresses but of gray
> spines . . . All of the doomed children together en-
> ter the range of the rhythm, a slight easing of the
> harshness is provided by making the flute sound for
> the rats like a real flute (unadulterated, unrelieved,
> fatal realism), whereas for the children it is meta-
> morphosed, calling to them like a trumpet (uncon-
> sciously, in the sound of the rhythm: *tra-ra-ra*).

So much is distilled here. And this alchemical solution pours out, in the case of the two Russians, as if waiting for a catalyst. And that in this case is the letter itself: the least trivial or compromised of forms, replete with confession and criticism, written for each other's gaze. Pasternak and Tsvetayeva discuss this quite a bit and she comes down on him hard for attempting to be a man of his time with his *Lieutenant Schmidt*. "Boris, everything is perfectly clear to me now: what I want is for Schmidt to say nothing. Schmidt to say nothing and you to say all . . . don't think I meant your entire *Schmidt* (the poem): I only meant the theme, your *tragic faithfulness* to the original" (my emphasis). She believes his greatest mistake was using the real Schmidt's letters, that this was a gesture of self immolation. "It's a pity . . . that you chose a hero of our times (timeless times) rather than a hero of ancient times, or, to put it more precisely (now quoting Stepun): a victim of dreaming instead of a hero of our dreams."

In return, his criticism notes her use of *detail*, a term that he imbued with tremendous import: "But in the physics of poetry you are always far more successful in dealing with the 'infinitely great' (definitions, sentiments philosophical ideas) than with the 'infinitely small' (the root of a quality, the tonality of an image, its uniqueness, etc.) . . . I have already remarked that in this poem you made a more careful selection of *detail* than you usually do." This assessment is only fitting and appropriate for a poet who was capable of lines of such delicacy and precision as "rain wrapped the fields in the quiet threads of assiduous drops," and "thunder/took off its cap and snapped/a hundred blinding photographs"—the poet who wrote:

> You ask who commands?
> Almighty God of detail,
> Almighty God of lovers . . .

> I don't know if they've solved
> the riddle of the dark beyond the grave,
> but life is like this silence:
> autumnal, particular.

Commenting on her work to Pasternak, Tsvetayeva reveals why she's not only difficult to translate but also why the American or English reader may not "get it." The edge of satire and grotesquerie in her work, the combination of tones (merging of the high and the low), the sense of always speaking directly and at a slant, the ferocity—she has Dickinson's quickness with more body.

> A single post, a point of rusting
>   tin in the sky
> marks the fated place we
>   move to, he and I

> on time   as death is
>   prompt   strangely
> too smooth the gesture of
>   his hat to me

> menace at the edges of his
>   eyes   his mouth tight
> shut   strangely too low is the
>   bow he makes tonight

> on time?
> ("Poem of the End," translated by Elaine Feinstein)

Though she doesn't rely on description of local color or scene, there's a rigorous and subtle phenomonology of place in her poems. And, she says, with astonishing directness, precisely what she means at all times, making her even more difficult to translate than her contemporaries. To which statement we can hear her response: "Writing poetry is in itself translating, from the mother tongue into another, whereas French or German should make no difference. *No language is the mother tongue.* Writing poetry is rewriting it. That's why I am puzzled when people talk of French or Russian, etc., poets" (my emphasis). Her meaning resides in her tone of voice, her manner of address, how she says and unsays. She is classical, terse, quick, elliptical: on a tightrope. (Elaine Feinstein's translations convey the last three aspects of her work quite well.)

Pasternak's tone, on the other hand, is an inversion of Kafka's. Consistent if bizarre. Maniacal. Nothing ghostly or ambiguous informs his presentation of self. He didn't lack self knowledge, but he could throw up his hands at the results of his self-analysis. "There are *thousands* of women whom I would have to love if I let myself go. I am ready to run after any manifestation of femininity, and my mind swarms with such visions. Perhaps I was born with this trait so that my character would be formed by the development of a strong, almost unfailing system of brakes." Lucid about the barricades and structures he has to erect around his own susceptible "feminine" nature, he doesn't plan to do anything about it. "My qualities as compared with his (Nikolai Tikhonov's) must be called maidenly, not merely feminine . . . . Perhaps you don't know what I'm talking about? About the terrible influence

wielded over me by appearances, chimeras, probabili-
ties, moods, and fantasies." The forms of imprisonment
he acknowledges are most often personal: wife, a child,
circumstances having to do with commissions.

But the invitation is here for us to reinvent, invigo-
rate, infuse these forms with meaning. "One rarely meets
with lyric poetry these days. But this is the main thing:
it is being heard again almost without any intermedi-
ary, more or less directly. This is extraordinary, this is
a happiness which in our circumstances is inexplicable
. . ."

In the battle against repression, it is letters like these
that show how the soul works its way out of the underground. The effect is doubly invigorating because
these poets weren't interested in escaping suffering,
only tyranny. They viewed suffering, whatever its result, as a high privilege: Reserved for humans. After
summarizing her rift with Pasternak, how she broke
the spell, Tsvetayeva concludes, ten years before she
will take her own life in Yelubuga: "Now everything
is all right, the realms separated: I in the innermost
self-outermost foreign place—quite out of the world."

FROM STROUDSBURG IN EARLY SPRING:
SOME THOUGHTS ON LETTERS AND POETRY

We've rented a house sight unseen for the month of April in Eastern Pennsylvania. We will be here eight, maybe nine days, interspersed through the month. We know no one in the area, and nothing about it. Writing a letter is a form of company. Letters are a way of commemorating the times when habits are forced to fall away.

Something about this experience is blessed. We arrive on Easter/Passover weekend. When we finally get the door open in the dark, my son's first words as he scans the floor are, "What a beautiful house!"

I bring with me a letter I received three days ago from a friend in another part of Pennsylvania and saved to savor in the woods, not that I anticipate things I want to hear but that a two-page single-spaced letter is a rarity in my life at this time and I want to read between its lines.

I want to tell her about the peculiar discontinuities of the place, the absence of any sign of industry, the signs for Shooting Ranges and the Paradise Trout Hatchery where you can get your pond or table stocked, about the abundance of Funeral Parlors and Honeymoon Cottages. Everywhere there's the sound of water murmuring. Streams stop and start without warning: one stream runs right

up to a barn door. She will think it's funny that the
house is set behind Frey's Funeral Parlor, or will she?
Maybe she'll interpret it as a sign of gloom, morbid-
ity, more thoughts about my father's death.

I want to tell her of how I try to search my memory
for what they do with dead animals on roadsides in
rural areas. On the road to Stroudsburg there's a dead
dog's eviscerated ribcage; a demolished porcupine's quills
still stand on end. Does their presence have something
to do with it being Easter Weekend?

In Stroudsburg we go to swim at the Y and everyone
huddled in the sauna is still in sweat clothes and ath-
letic shoes. It's over 200 degrees and after five minutes I'm ready to leave, but not before I overhear a
stocky, muscular woman saying that she must lose eight
pounds today to join the Marines tomorrow. She is
addressing a black man who turns out to be a Marine
Sergeant. He's drenched in sweat. I ask him how long
he will stay here. "An hour and a half," he answers,
"with breaks." I ask him how he can take it. He looks
at me nonplussed. "I'm just trying to break a sweat."

My desire to inform and amuse my friend is waning.

I have brought with me to La Anna a book by Cioran,
The Trouble with Being Born, because I know I can read
its strangled thoughts in stray moments. I open it at
random, read a passage, and immediately feel exoner-
ated. "Some of the *Provincial Letters* were rewritten as
many as seventeen times. Astounding that Pascal could
have expended so much time and energy whose interest seems minimal to us now. Every polemic dates—
every polemic with men."

The four great poet letter writers of this century are Rainer Maria Rilke, D.H. Lawrence, Boris Pasternak, and Marina Tsvetayeva. In their hands the letter can be the least trivial or artificial or compromised of forms. And in 1926 Rilke, Pasternak, and Tsvetayeva corresponded with each other. In one of her last letters to Rilke, Tsvetayeva writes: "What have I seen of life? Throughout my youth (from 1917 on)—black toil, Moscow? Prague? Paris? St.-Gilles? Same thing. Always stove, broom, money (none)."

Some letters are a form of monologue, dress rehearsals for works to come. Their freshness and spontaneity are crucial. Poetry needs to make the private language of the letter public, but not by changing the information, just ordering and shading it differently. We cannot write to someone whose life holds no mystery for us. Every quality of a letter is inseparable from the person to whom it is addressed. In poetry the addressee prevents eloquence from degenerating into rhetoric or patter. No matter how direct the presentation of things— the sea, the rocks, the light—it's all glintings and intimation: the central idea need not be stated and yet is everywhere present.

Pasternak's letters are as rich and oblique and metonymic as his poetry. He shows us how to abandon a subject, how we can, by fearlessly attributing the character of our moods to things apart from us, get them to speak back, to return our gaze, repay our acts of attention. And so the thing beheld becomes the beholder: the man doesn't look at the tree, the tree looks at the man "with a thousand noisy eyes" ("Spring"); it sees him. He sought clarity without simplification. When he writes

to his cousin Olga Friedenburg about how he reacted
to the shock of their separation, he puts it from the
street's perspective: "I wanted to tell you a tale about
the city limits, about the outskirts where I found myself at that very moment, where the street, such a simple
macadam street, so used to itself, to being cramped by
its crust—where this street, I say, simple and ordinary
in the center of town, suffers the shock of having to
take leave of the great highways at the town's end,
where it waves clouds of dust to the horizon at the far
end of a long green leash and, still echoing the town,
changes its nature, becoming sentimental in a one-sto-
ried, wooden-framed way meant to express extreme
tenderness."

The best letters to receive are usually the most difficult ones to answer. We recoil from them. Like masterpieces, they can depress or overwhelm us. Confu-
sion may result, misunderstandings multiply. *A* will
think that Z is angry at him because he never responded
to his letter, something he said offended, when in fact
Z could not rouse himself to respond *in kind*, adequately,
to *A*'s points.

The responder apologizes because he is late in reply-
ing. . . . But this only seems to be the case. The apol-
ogy embodies a deeper severance from others and their
needs because the writer did not feel impelled to re-
ply and so he didn't until motivated by the desire not
to hurt through his silence. Such hesitation never impedes those who are immersed in a correspondence, a
dialogue, in which the writer's freedom is ramified.
Hesitation, where letters end, is where poems begin to
be born.

The telephone has no more killed the letter than "the railway, according to this mode of thinking, was destined to kill contemplation," Proust remarks. We are not strangers to the mode of thinking that, in trying to make art progress along the lines of science, in speaking of "time saving devices," is always asserting the inevitable loss of this or that aspect of art, of artifice. Now we take a train when we're not in a hurry to get where we're going and we cherish letters for similar reasons, for what they can deliver apart from useful information.

When Shelley arrived somewhere he would sit down immediately and write a ten page letter to, say, Hogg. This was his way of stirring up the depths. And many of his poems preserve the spontaneity of their first impulse, the archetypal plaint of letters.

> You are not here! the quaint witch Memory sees,
> In vacant chairs, your absent images,
> And points where you once sat, and now should be
> But are not.
> > ("Letter to Maria Gisborne")

Wordsworth wrote "Tintern Abbey" when his carriage stopped above the Abbey and the river Wye. Auden refers to such travelers ruefully in *Letter to Lord Byron*,

> I am no Lawrence who, on his arrival,
> > Sat down and typed out all he had to say;
> I am not even Ernest Hemingway.

Rilke wrote the *Duino Elegies* (with that long interval between the first two and the rest) and *Sonnets to Orpheus* as quickly as he once wrote letters to the Princess von Thurn. He waited ten years (if a number can ever be attached to that kind of time), lived his life for something he did in a matter of days.

Writing letters and writing poems have this in common: one can never remember having written them. One remembers the circumstances surrounding their composition, not the writing. They both swallow up the time in which they were written.

Some letters which begin with apologies are often instances of reluctant eloquence. Proust wrote to Jacques Rivière to apologize for not writing an essay on Baudelaire and then went on in his most deft and exquisite style to touch on all of Baudelaire's qualities that he would have liked to have discussed, "En Passant." The result is a model of what an essay might be if the writer had the courage to approach it with abandon, absolute (involuntary) candor. The movement of Proust's mind, rejecting its own participation, stopping and starting, but always against the pressure of reluctance, resisting, always resisting, finds an example that corresponds to its specific ambivalence, dredges up, in passing, exactly what might have been lost in a more willful performance, "Un éclaire . . . puis la nuit!"

Why are the beginnings of books (especially the introductions to books that set out to develop theories) usually the best part? There are many reasons, but by no means the least of them is that the desire to say is still keen, and the ideas are still potent. Most of these books, many of which have provocative titles, go on to say nothing more than is latent in the proposed topic. Insights liberate and incite further thought. Constructs constrict.

One doesn't write a letter, as it were, "surrounded by books." No one can write with abandon while worrying about correct quotations and footnotes. This kind of double thinking can not only disrupt the flow of writing, it can destroy the mind that may forget how to trust itself and lose track of its first impulses forever. This is the price the academic writer, who has traded liberty for library, may have to pay for accuracy.

George Seferis, whose diplomatic chores often kept him from writing, looked forward to finishing "Thrush" during an island retreat. He later felt that only because he forgot his "notes" that he was finally driven to compose the poem he had planned.

Criticism has much to relearn from letters. Writers will say in letters what they would never own up to in print for fear of repercussions. It is important, as with dreams, that these thoughts just be written down— they don't all have to be developed.

Sartre was willing to risk his credibility in the dazzling *Search for a Method*, the introduction to the *Critique of Dialectical Reason*, by stating that the problem of scarcity no longer exists, that world hunger can be solved now by technological means. And then he proceeds in successively unreadable volumes to discuss the impossibly complicated implications while the reader is still gasping in the wheel-tracks of this simple, shattering, hopeful (if true!) truth.

A biography by Samuel Johnson, by today's standards, is a mere letter, a proposal. He is said to have written the *Life of Savage* in thirty-six hours. One can hear the modern publisher telling Johnson after reading his *Life of Milton*: "Wonderful! Now you're ready to begin."

Le mot juste and free association: letters show us a route around these two detours.

Letters are the province of minor illnesses. Poetry is about waiting, letters are about filling up the time, notating.

How many letters begin with the weather? It is for the difference between days that we turn to poetry. The weather is the wild card on the poet's palette.

> Here the weather remains the same.
>   Constant summer
> sun. When was the sky anything but blue?
>   (Stephen Dobyns, "Letter Beginning with the First
>   Line of Your Letter")

The modernists turned the weather into a code. They wrote poetry with spiritual tone that (with exceptions) makes no explicit reference to the inner life. Shallow dislocations mimic deeper ones; the little shifts in the surface signal deeper disturbances.

Weather changes violently in early spring. The weather in Stroudsburg is unseasonably cold. Our neighbors predicted we'd see snow again before April was finished. A trickle of hailstones accompanies our first and last walk around a pond.

At what point does the poet want to differentiate his poem from prose? Often after readings people remark that the poet's comments leading up to the poem were better than the poem. Better? More fulsome? Anecdotal? The poem begins where experience leaves off. The poet plies his art against the grain of the experience and tries to heed Eliot's warning not to fall into the trap of having the experience but missing the meaning.

Auden and Elizabeth Bishop and Frank O'Hara are masters of the letter poem. Auden is most himself in *Letter to Lord Byron*.

> I want a form that's large enough to swim in,
>   And talk on any subject that I choose,
> From natural scenery to men and women
>   Myself, the arts, the European news:

Bishop tells of having tried to write a villanelle all her life but being unable to finish one until, in writing "One Art," "it was like writing a letter." She derived something of her intimate tone from the precedent Auden had set. Casualness was a fast way to get around all the impasses set up by modernist poetics: the impersonal poet adrift in a history where all time is coterminous.

By the time we reach Frank O'Hara the only time that exists is the present and the time is noted as the date would be in a letter.

Charles Olson's poems and letters often originated as letters. That's why they sometimes read as a kind of shorthand.

Just before Richard Hugo began writing letter poems his work had reached a point where he could say anything, where he could counterpoint the mundane ("even the tuna salad in Reedpoint tastes good") and the profound with a subtlety and deviousness that demanded re-reading. "Pray hard to weather," he urged, "that lone surviving god/that in some sudden wisdom we surrender." The poems in *Lady in the Kicking Horse Reservoir* were like snapshots with the shutter left open long enough for duration to enter the frame. He was direct, but he glimpsed things from odd angles. He managed the high wire act of being talky without garrulousness; his line stayed taut, and mystery emerged in an unforced way: "Fields that never meant/a lover harm slant eerie, and the next town/promises no language or a stove." There was as much sage as sage in his poems. But paradoxically the casual candor dispersed once he began to write intentional epistolary poems. The long drives through ghost towns he would never enter had given him a necessary distance from his subject. He needed an anti-mask, not a mask that fit his face.

It is this right tone that is so hard to locate in poems that move us. No one has devised a way of talking about tone: It has to do with intention being understood without needing to be underscored.

Keats said something to this effect in a letter to Reynolds: "We hate poetry that has a palpable design upon us." All of Keats' great insights appear in letters written to sympathetic friends. He never set out after a generalized truth; he happened upon them and moved on.

Imagine poems that are as sprightly and diverse as Keats' letters and as inwardly formed, innerscaped, as his Odes.

Many of Byron's letters are touched by a delicious absurdity. He is not all gloom and ribaldry. His intelligence would not let him alone. His letters, like those of Keats, are further documents propelling poetry toward immediacy and inclusiveness and free verse.

Could Pope hope for a better defense than the one Byron gives him in a letter to John Murray? "I will show more imagery in twenty lines of Pope than in any equal length of quotations in English poesy, and that in places where they least expect it: for instance, in his lines on Sporus—now, do just read them over—the subject is of no consequence (whether it be Satire or Epic)—we are talking of *poetry* and *imagery from* Nature *and* Art."

The letters of Keats and Byron are better than all but their best work.

Walden is like a letter; its tone is best described as *bordering on*. It is the most secret American book: personal essay, mythic tale, journal, prose poem. The book is an indirect, ironic revision of Emerson's high-minded sermons. Thoreau assumes an intimacy with his reader which allows for a private humor of which others may readily understand the gist if not the particulars. He is mischievous; he chips away at the reader's resistances. "I have a great deal of company in my house; especially in the morning, when nobody calls."

Whitman also posits a reader both immediate and waiting on the precipice of the future. "What I shall assume you shall assume." He too takes on the role of responding to Emerson by making him concrete.

What Thoreau and Whitman do with Emerson is similar to what Marx does with Hegel: they put theory into practice; provide a kind of ballast.

When my son was about two he would break into my room, make a run on the typewriter and start banging the keys. Reluctantly assuming a straight face, I would say, "Not now, I'm *wor*king." But he would find his way back when I was no longer there, and take over the typewriter. If I interrupted his arhythmic banging of the keys he would assume a solemn expression and cool distant voice to match it: "No. I'm wor-king," casting me in the role of Emerson, the straight man, the one who lays down the rules.

Bob Dylan gives wonderful mention to the letter as metaphor for miscommunication:

> Yes I received your letter yesterday
> About the time the doorknob broke
> When you asked me how I was doing
> Is that some kind of joke.
> ("Desolation Row")

Letters are written quickly and (one hopes) not revised. They are most notable for what they leave out. The letter form allows the writer to complete a thought in one sitting. And not explain it.

Poets do their best work when they catch themselves off guard, when everything that they thought they had prepared to write falls by the wayside.

Tranströmer calls his long poem *Baltics* "a long letter to the dead/on a typewriter that doesn't have a ribbon, only a horizon line/so the words beat in vain and nothing stays." This urgency, this sense of his work always being, to appropriate Frank O'Hara's phrase, "meditations in an emergency," is what generates the form and the style of his work—quick observation crisscrossed by aphorism. What is said is inseparable from the moment of its utterance.

> A letter from America drove me out again,
>   started me walking . . .
> among newborn districts without memories,
>   cool as blueprints.
>
> Letter in my pocket. Half-mad, lost walking,
>   it is a kind of prayer.
> Out there evil and good actually have faces.
> For the most part with us it's a fight between
>   roots, numbers, shades of light.
> ("Out in the Open," translated by Robert Bly)

Tranströmer (psychologist by profession) has always had little time to write, but this is the situation of most poets. It is the attitude of having little time that helps the mind seek out and find congenial forms. The letter in his pocket allows him to fantasize a kind of opposition, a place (America) where distinctions are clear—black and white. But this is how we tend to perceive anything that is not ours. Gray is the color of habit; poetry begins with a rupture of routine.

I continue with my letter to my friend from Stroudsburg,
knowing I will not mail it: "But the rooms are mysteriously the right size. Whatever that means. Whatever
that might mean. The light is not pouring in the windows. The light stays where it has fallen. It hangs on
the brink of radiance."

As I was riding the bus to Mitla and gazing at the graded, layered mountain ranges, and the peasant plowing the field with two white oxen next to a disused tractor, I thought of how few works of art really stayed with me. And I remembered the injunction of Malcolm Lowry's contemporary Cyril Connolly, in *Enemies of Promise*, that an artist's sole responsibility was to create a masterpiece and that nothing else was worthwhile.

The way to go about writing a masterpiece is not necessarily by fixing the locus of the pressure on each line of a poem or each sentence of a novel. But Hart Crane and Malcolm Lowry consumed and tormented themselves daily with this task and considered themselves to be failures: not failures in comparison to their contemporaries, but in relation to the work which they had planned but could not execute. This would not be such a delicate and difficult matter had they not each produced masterpieces, works head and heels above those of their less ambitious, somewhat "saner," more tractable contemporaries, like Graham Greene and Archibald MacLeish. These works were masterpieces which they knew they could never exceed, only equal. (Yes, Crane might write a long poem that bettered *The Bridge*, but could he better, *on their own terms*, his best short and shorter poems, like "Legend," "Black Tambourine," "Repose of Rivers," "My Grandmother's Love Letters," "Praise for an Urn," and "O Carib Isle"?) Perhaps it was this sense of failure they were trying to assuage which took the form of a thirst—a thirst alcohol only magnified.

*

The conflicts of a life show up on the litmus of form. I pose the question: did the "problems" of Hart Crane and Malcolm Lowry result more from accumulated desperation, or from a failure to find, in the long run (and for it), significant forms as artists? Or, to put it another way, did Crane and Lowry drink as they did because they were mysteriously tormented, battered inwardly by sexual confusions and unremitting longings for something more than "existence as *sold*" to them (Lowry's phrase, my emphasis), or because, as artists, or poets and novelists, they failed to find forms that allowed them *to go on* without extended blockage, hiatus?

*

Hart Crane went to Mexico in 1932 on a Guggenheim Fellowship ostensibly to write a history of Mexico in verse: a spectacularly unrealistic project. He barely had time to get settled and write letters and a few poems before the year was out.

Malcolm Lowry (following in Crane's footsteps and aware of Ambrose Bierce's mysterious disappearance) wrote most of *Under the Volcano* in Mexico and conceived a trilogy (*The Voyage that Never Ends*) to rival Proust, Joyce, Mann and Musil in its architectonic complexity.

*

What drew Lowry and Crane to Mexico? Certainly one reason was that it was possible to live more cheaply on a modest income there than in the United States or Europe: Crane could stretch his fellowship and Lowry his small allowance from his father.

Mexico offered "a collective desolate fecundity," which Lowry sought and Crane evoked in his last and perhaps greatest poem, "The Broken Tower."

Mexico was a kind of solution to the problem Henri Lefebvre sets forth in *Everyday Life in the Modern World*: "our aim is to prove that a system of everyday life (in America and Europe) does not exist, notwithstanding all the endeavours to establish and settle it for good and all, and that there are only sub-systems separated by irreducible gaps, yet situated on one plane and related to it."

*

I have been walking for days in Oaxaca, the valley of the acacias. As you go higher, the town thins out and the air gets clearer. Each day I climb a little farther into the hills. I watch the clouds darken over the mountains. There's the sense of a city in flotation, of a place not fully of the world, a presence bordering on the magical, the marginal. The architecture is not so different now from what it was 500 years before. Steep streets sweep downward toward the zocalo and upward toward the mountains, mountains that hold the valley gently, mountains that build up the wall of the sky. There's mystery in the play of light-shadow over the landscape.

In the evening, we go to a Spanish restaurant whose balcony overlooks the zocalo. A demonstration which had been going on in the streets all day, on the Avenues Juarez and Constitution, has moved to the center of town. They are demonstrating for more money for teachers and freedom of expression: ¡Viva La Libertad de Expresión! As we watch the demonstrators congregate, the sky turns black, lightning begins to flicker in the hills above the city and thunder rumbles. It is as dark and ominous a sky as I have ever seen. It would have needed an El Greco or Albert Pinkham Ryder to do it justice. But the demonstrators seem oblivious to the symbolism of the weather and in spite of the imminent deluge, continue to shout through megaphones.

*

Outside the bus depot of the Hotel Meson del Angel a dark-eyed child is bottle-feeding an infant. She looks up as if to say, do you think I was born to do this? The woman beside her on the street has set out half a dozen straw baskets brimful with dark roots and branches.

*

How advanced the Mayans and the Olmecs and the Zapotecs were. The mounds are still under excavation as we walk over them.

Each instant another minute layer is uncovered as if these vast tumuli were metaphors for the process of knowing—always partially—our own minds.

The myriad maize and rain-gods seated like Buddhas; the mad, wild, expressive faces; the decorated skulls drilled all the way through.

Do the images on the stele arise from where the Indians settled? *In* the valley, *on* the mountain?

The beautiful place-names of the ruins: the ones with the soft x-sounds, like Uxmal; the ones with the drawn out ch- and tz-sounds, like Chichén-Itzá. Ruins are replete with steps that lead nowhere. Dusty side streets veer off into the blinding light; stretch through roofless houses and houses that are only roofs.

The poppy-red blossoms on the jacaranda trees.

*

Mexico is exotic; it's a culture that still has celebrations, outlets for the inner, darker self; it offers release from the fixity of worldly identity—the name attached to the face. Everyday life is at times a celebration, a festival, even a festival for the dead.

Travel in Mexico is like the feista: while it opens you up it also wounds.

Mexico provides a perverse twist on traditional values. When a plan to share a house with friends in Cuernavaca fell through in the spring of 1970, I decided to go to Mexico anyway.

I went with a woman I scarcely knew, but was fiercely attracted to. We were en route to Mexico City, from where we'd catch a bus to Cuernavaca, when I changed my mind in midair, changed the destination of our tickets when we stopped to change planes in Austin, and went on to Puerto Vallarta instead, to begin the summer in some proximity to the sea after the year in the city.

Why Puerto Vallarta? Once, returning from Mazatlán
to Los Angeles with my father, we changed planes at
a small airport with a single runway. I had no sooner
walked a few steps past the "terminal" hut than I was
in the jungle. Vines from the nearby trees choked the
gutters under the eaves. A brash, arrogant film-crew
stomped through, en route to "Puerto Vallarta"—the
place-name hung in the air like a song named after a
town, "Cordoba," or "Laredo." I asked my father where
it was, what it was like. "Now that *was* a paradise,"
he said, and I trusted his judgment though I knew he'd
never been there, "but now it's ruined." He thought I
was slow, and I was: I just couldn't grasp how a paradise could be ruined *overnight* because some movie had
been shot there. The movie took it off the map for him,
and the name of the town remained in the back of my
mind as a place I would have to see for myself some
day, just to see it.

In Puerto Vallarta the sea blazed. In one torrential summer
rain, I huddled in a doorway and saw some children
cutting the tail off an iguana. And one afternoon, while
I was walking aimlessly on the sun-baked main street,
two barely disguised plain-clothes cops, dressed in a
Hawaiian shirts and light-colored polyester slacks with
pockets bulging just below their shirttails, requested
to see my passport which I'd left back at the top-floor
villa apartment we'd rented dirt cheap.

This gave the cops an excuse to inspect the apartment.
One of them unearthed, in the top drawer of the dresser,
unhidden, a penis-shaped wooden hash pipe, from which
he dislodged a few specks of tar. I decided on this
story, which, as it turned out, was neither a good nor

a bad tactic and which may or may not have been the full truth: "I had hoped to score some hash in Mexico, but once I discovered it was illegal, I decided not to."

His silent, reactive, mime-like partner came across a copy of the Bible, a new translation of the Old Testament my stepfather had given me and which I'd brought along to study Ezekiel—to help myself better understand Blake and Eliot.

They exchanged solumn, sincere glances. "Do you read this?" "Yes." They looked at me now with no uncertain respect. I could sense our fortunes were turning, but still feared incarceration in a Mexican jail. From the way the first cop squinched his features and grimaced, I thought they might take the pipe, issue me a warning, and split. But no, they decided to leave my fate up to the Captain.

It seemed wet as a cave inside the Captain's office in the jail where I was seated in a straight-backed chair facing his desk. I sat up very straight. In his blues, the Captain at least looked like a cop. There was no excess flesh on his bones. Everything about him said: no nonsense.

"Des ees hash," he said, tapping out another tarred speck from the pipe. "It's just tar," I said, "and it's been there for a long time. Someone gave me that pipe in New York." "No. I say ees hash. I could throw you in jail right now."

He looked up at the first cop to corroborate his findings. The first cop leaned over and whispered something in the Captain's ear.

"My man tells me you read the Bible." "All the time,
sir, all the time." "All right, since this is all we found . . .
youcangothistime," he said, running the words together
as he rose to shake my hand.

*

It is always tempting to look at the crises of writers in
light of their personal histories. The lives concern me
here *only* as they intersect with the art. Crane and Lowry
were both deeply estranged from their families, offspring of wealthy businessmen who were unreachable.

Crane was moving toward a reconciliation with his father who died when he was in Mexico. This manufac-
turer of the "Life Saver" was no fool—he wrote Hart
that "The River" was the best thing he had done. Hart's
relationship with his mother was an emotional catastrophe.

Lowry abandoned any hope of intimacy with his father as a teenager and, before consenting to go to Cambridge,
shipped out as a deck hand on a tramp steamer. At 19
he wrote and asked Conrad Aiken to serve *in loco parentis.*
His first letter to his literary hero ("I know you are a
great man in your own country") has the feel of "Après
le Déluge" and shows what Lowry could do right from
the start when he wasn't pressing:

> I have lived only nineteen years and all of them more
> or less badly. [He quotes from Aiken's "The House
> of Dust."] I sat opposite the Bureau-de-change. The
> great gray tea urn perspired. But as I read, I became
> conscious only of a blur of faces: I let the tea that
> had mysteriously appeared grow clammy and milk-

starred, the half veal and ham pie remain in its crinkly paper; vaguely, as though she had been speaking upon another continent, I heard the girl opposite me order some more Dundee cake. My pipe went out.

. . . The sunlight roared above me like a vast invisible sea. The crowd of faces wavered and broke and flowed. . . . Sometime when you come to London, Conrad Aiken, wilst hog it over the way somewhere with me? You will forgive my presumption, I think, in asking you this.

*

Disaster dogged Lowry's heels every step of the way. He lost the suitcase that contained the manuscript for his first novel, *Ultramarine*, and had to reconstitute the book from notes. To write *Lunar Caustic* he checked himself into Bellevue and then was "mistaken" (like the Pulitzer hungry journalist in Samuel Fuller's *Shock Corridor*) for one of the mad. It was fifteen years before his second novel, *Under the Volcano*, appeared. His squatter's shack in Canada went up in flames, consuming his magnum opus in progress, *The Voyage that Never Ends*.

The contradictions, the inevitable failure of Crane's verse epic already lay in the tortured history of Mexico itself, in the heart of the very problem he intended to wrestle with: the conquest. Unable to reconcile himself to his project, unable to ply contradiction as "a lever of transcendence" (Simone Weil) Crane leapt into the sea, into oneness.

As silent as a mirror is believed
Realities plunge in silence by . . .

Lowry's suicide was more ambiguous. He didn't exactly intend to kill himself, and his death was labeled Death by Misadventure. While on a walking tour of England (always dangerous inflammatory ground for him), he and his wife had a fight, and he swallowed booze and pills, perhaps not enough to kill him in themselves, but a bad enough combination to make him choke on his own vomit. This eruption seemed all the more cruel in that it followed the healing years in Canada with Margerie, all the work he had done on himself toward a fresh start—for which no one had ever been more willing.

> One evening on the way back from the spring for some reason I suddenly thought of a break by Bix in Frankie Trumbauer's record of Singing the Blues that had always seemed to me to express a moment of the most pure spontaneous happiness. I could never hear this break without feeling happy myself and wanting to do something good. Could one translate this kind of happiness into one's life? Since this was only a moment of happiness I seemed involved with irreconcilable impulses. One could not make a moment permanent and perhaps the attempt to try was some form of evil. But was there not some means of suggesting at least the existence of such happiness, that was like what is really meant by freedom, which was like the spring, which was like our love, which was like the desire to be truly good.
>
> ("The Forest Path to the Spring")

*

Crane and Lowry were unwilling to make any concession to what Frost praised in Wordsworth—"necessary dullness." Everything had to be a monumental under-

taking or it wasn't worth doing. (Monumental and coherent, like [theoretically] *Ulysses*.)

Though drawn to grandiose schemes with cosmic implications, they were both writers of consciousness, not
of history. Crane's imagination was synthetic, not dialectical. Lowry said that any defect in *Under the Volcano* sprang from "something irremediable in the author's
equipment" that was—he confessed with remarkable
candor in his letter of appeal to his publisher, Jonathan
Cape—

> subjective rather than objective, a better equipment,
> in short, for a certain kind of poet than a novelist.

*

Crane was the kind of man who would allow himself
to become converted by a book, and more fierce in his
defense of an idea that bloodied him than the author
might have been. The most nervous moment in Crane's
letters is when he undertakes to read Spengler.

Eliot may have written, exploded and secreted actually, at different times, *The Waste Land*, because it was
a poem he had to write, but Crane interpreted the act
as another of Eliot's definitive demonstrations of how
the individual talent should incorporate tradition: one
had to mix the symbolic and the real, the modern and
the ancient, in such and such a way. Crane is at his
most Eliot-like in "General Aims and Theories" when
he writes of what he set out to do in "For the Marriage of Faustus and Helen,"

> to embody in modern terms (words, symbols, meta-
> phors) a contemporary approximation to an ancient

human culture or mythology . . . build . . . a bridge
between the so-called classic experience and many
divergent realities of our seething, confused cosmos
of today, which has no formulated mythology yet
for classic poetic reference or for religious exploitation . . .

Some passages in the poem accomplish this desired
synthesis, ("I found 'Helen' in a street car"):

> And yet, suppose some evening I forgot
> The fare and transfer, yet got by that way
> Without recall,—lost yet poised in traffic.
> Then I might find your eyes across an aisle,
> Still flickering with those prefigurations—
> Prodigal, yet uncontested now,
> Half-riant before the jerky window frame.

But later, in the midst of struggling with *The Bridge*,
Crane would pay the price for having taken Eliot straight.

*

Crane and Lowry created the myths by which they are
judged. Their great works are not failures: they are
great works.

Crane and Lowry found apt objectifications in the bridge,
the bell tower, and the two volcanoes, Popocateptl and
Ixtaccihuatl. But in their respective use of Brooklyn
Bridge and the volcanoes they came dangerously close
to placing the symbol OVER the real.

> O harp and alter, of the fury fused,
> (How could mere toil align thy choiring strings!)
> . . .

Ixtaccihuatl and Popocatepetl, that image of the perfect marriage, lay now clear and beautiful on the horizon under an almost pure morning sky. Far above
him a few white clouds were racing windily after a
pale gibbous moon. Drink all morning, they said to
him, drink all day. This is life!

*

What are the artistic consequences of employing an
aesthetic that goes against the grain of one's gifts? Structure
becomes external. Technique becomes an overriding concern.
Joyce and Eliot and Kafka rarely mention adopting techniques
(the latter had contempt for Apollinaire's "pyrotech-
nics" in "Zone"). But Crane and Lowry obsessed about
structure and technique all the time. They were both
eclectic, consciously cadging montage from John Dos
Passos and William Carlos Williams. This from Crane's
"The River":

> Stick your patent name on a signboard
> brother—all over—going west—young man
> Tintex—Japalac—Certain-teed Overalls ads
> and lands sakes! under the new playbill ripped
> in the guaranteed corner—see Bert Williams what?

These passages from *Under the Volcano:*

> DAILY GLOBE *intelube londres presse collect follow-*
> *ing yesterdays headcoming antisemitic campaign mexpress*
> *propetition see tee emma mexworkers confederation proexpulsion*
> *exmexico quote small jewish textile manufacturers unquote*
> *twas learned today per-reliable source that german lega-*
> *tion mexcity actively behind . . .*

> The dehydrated onion factory by the sidings awoke,
> then the coal companies. *It's a black business but we*

use you white: Daemon's Coal . . . A delicious smell of onion soup in sidestreets of Vavin impregnated the early morning.

Lowry found new uses for montage in a literary work, as when the poster for the film *Las Manos de Orlac* (The Hands of Orlac), playing in Quahnahuac on the day in which the novel takes place, reappears at strategic moments in the book, and it becomes, by extension, (as every such repeated image does in *Under the Volcano*), a symbol of the book itself. *Orlac* symbolizes the Consul's misuse of his powers; he becomes a kind of black magician, another double within the book's plethora of doubles.

> Yet what a complicated endless tale it seemed to tell, of tyranny and sanctuary, that poster looming above him now, showing the murderer Orlac! An artist with a murderer's hands; that was the ticket, the hieroglyphic of the times. For really it was Germany itself that, in the gruesome degradation of a bad cartoon, stood over him.—Or was it, by some uncomfortable stretch of the imagination, M. Laruelle himself?

In *Las Manos de Orlac*, a pianist, whose hands are somehow (I have never seen it) ruined by a train accident has a murderer's hands sewn on by an evil doctor Gogol. And so the pianist, in good doppelgänger fashion, becomes a murderer against his conscious will. I think Lowry was drawn to this tale because he liked the idea of an external agent being the cause.

For a more immediate sense of what *The Hands of Orlac* was really like, I must look to another of Lowry's doubles, Graham Greene, who reviewed *Orlac* (as *Mad Love*) during

his sojourn as a film critic while he was writing *The
Power and the Glory.*

> Guiltily I admit to liking Hands of Orlac because it
> did make me shudder a little when Dr. Gogol grafted
> the hands of a guillotined murderer onto the smashed
> stumps of Orlac, the great pianist whose hands had
> been destroyed in a railway accident, and because
> Herr Karl Freund's romantic direction did 'put across'
> the agreeable little tale of how the dead murderer's
> fingers retained a life of their own, the gift of knife-
> throwing, an inclination to murder. . . .

Even better is his praise of Peter Lorre:

> Those marbly pupils in the pasty spherical face are
> like the eye-pieces of a microscope through which
> you can see laid flat on the slide the entangled mind
> of a man: love and lust, nobility and perversity, ha-
> tred of itself and despair jumping out at you from
> the jelly.

*

The Consul, a shell of a man, must become no-man,
like Odysseus in the cave of the Cyclops, in order to
become himself again, and see things shorn of an alcoholic haze and heightening. Wandering through a
plaza with wooly nerves the Consul is drawn toward
a Ferris Wheel, a "little Popocatepetl":

> ¡BRAVA ATRACCIÓN!
>
> 10 c MÁQUINA INFERNAL

Again Lowry is throwing a little wink toward his own life. He asked his French translator, Mlle. Clarisse Francillon, if she could smuggle a copy of her translation to

> Jean Cocteau, and tell him I have never forgotten his kindness in giving me a seat for La Machine Infernale at the Champs Elysees in May, 1934. . . . And so you see his infernal machine comes back to torment the Consul in Chapter VII.

His worldly identity is wrested away from him as he is flung about and then hangs upside down in the grip of this "infernal machine," the sensation of falling "unlike-anything, beyond experience."

> Everything was falling out of his pockets, was being wrested from him, torn away, a fresh article at each whirling, sickening, plunging, retreating, unspeakable circuit, his notecase, pipe, keys, his dark glasses he had taken off, his small change he did not have time to imagine being pounced on by the children after all, he was being emptied out, returned empty, his stick, his passport—had that been his passport?

Lowry was a Cambridge educated Englishman living unmoored in the Third World. (He could not, like Graham Greene, change locales with each book.)

*

Both Crane and Lowry felt orphaned before they arrived in Mexico with its cult of orphans, "orphanos."

I remember walking, in the summer of 1970, across the courtyard of the orphanage in Guadalajara where José Clemente Orozco's great mural is housed. Walking, from the silence of that space into the maniacally kinetic howl of his work. (Better for it to be housed in an orphanage than in a church.) No one has rendered force more viscerally than Orozco, who harnessed the erotic shapes of surrealism and merged them with a cubist rigor. And fragmentation here provides its own quota of torque. My footsteps echoed. Where were the orphans?

Orozco shows not only the horrors of war, but the historical process through which the use of force becomes preeminent. Force permeates the living: the fuselage in the horse's belly makes him reel with agony. Orozco knew in his bones that the attempt to force Mexico into a European mold left a howl at the center, the cry of the orphaned, those whom, as Lowry would have said, "have nobody them with."

I was not prepared for what I had seen and longed to rest in the shadows under the colonnades.

*

The Third World/the desert—these are like a chemical mixture that magnifies and highlights the core of certain frustrations.

Nowhere is this anguish more apparent than in Antonioni's *The Passenger* when Jack Nicholson's character "Locke" falls to his knees in the sand beside his broken down Land Rover—it is a moment of ultimate, pure frustration, which mirrors his spiritual crisis. The desert, with its codes the reporter (Locke) cannot understand, cannot *process*, becomes a source of terror in which the mind can only break itself. The values of Western civilization are thrown into question by this world of silence, of eternal waiting. A man passes on a camel in a kind of final comment. Locke realizes that what he thought was true is only a partial truth, that what he took for reality is only part of reality, i.e.—a man in a Land Rover is essentially superior to a man on a camel. But in the desert this is not so.

*

Crane and Lowry were spiritually exiled from a literary community that had put aside the verbal rhetoric, the richness, and the grandeur they sought. They resented the limitation and constraints imposed upon them by the ethos of the time.

> Though tragedy was in the process of becoming unreal and meaningless it seemed one was still permitted to remember the days when an individual life held some value and was not a mere misprint in a communiqué.
>
> (*Under the Volcano*)

*

Most modernists were able to take for granted a vast storehouse of meaning and symbol which allowed them to stray, digress, and play, without evident strain. Their work is playful and confident and almost serene in spite of its "dark" themes.

Lowry and Crane tried to do with premeditation what Joyce and Eliot did with irony, panache, and nerve,

and neither trusted the spontaniety, the pulsing elec-
tric responsiveness which William Carlos Williams and
D.H. Lawrence employed—that submission to the process
of working itself.

Here's the catch. It could be argued that neither Williams nor Lawrence ever wrote a single poem or novels as great, as *finished*, as any of a dozen poems by
Crane or *Under the Volcano*, but nor were they "finished" by the writing of a work. One work cleared the
ground for the next work.

Even Proust "had not gone in search of the two uneven paving-stones upon which [he] stumbled." It was
the "fortuitous and inevitable fashion" in which this
occurred that showed him the truth of the past, and
how lost time could be retrieved, brought back to life.
His discovery has the force of a revelation which owes
everything to chance. "What we have not had to decipher," he writes, "to elucidate by our own efforts, what
was clear before we looked at it [plans, strategems,
symbols] is not ours."

*

Robert Lowell, whose work represents a bizarre fusion of elements in Crane and William Carlos Williams,
called Crane "the Shelley of our age." To enter the
realm of pure possibility for a moment, it seems to me
that Shelley has a poem, "Julian and Maddalo: A Conversation," that might have served as a model for Crane's
Mexican project. Formal discoveries are contextual as
well as metrical, and the graceful movement of Shelley's
poem has as much to do with the situation he creates
for his "characters" to engage in dialogue in their movement

through physical space as it does with his deft heroic couplets: a conversation between Julian and Maddalo is conducted—in an almost electrical sense—as they ride along the Venetian shores at dusk.

> So, as we rode, we talked; and the swift thought,
> Winging itself with laughter, lingered not,
> But flew from brain to brain—such glee was ours,
> Charged with light memories of remembered hours,
> None slow enough for sadness: till we came
> Homeward, which always makes the spirit tame.

The movement through imagined space draws our attention away from the closure of rhyme. "Julian and Maddalo" is as provisional as it is unwilled; it feels as if it wrote itself; it has the ballast—the gravity—most of Shelley's poems lack. But nothing has been lost in terms of aspiration—he has his eye on a moving object—from the "hillocks, heaped from ever-shifting sand" in the

> waste
> And solitary places; where we taste
> The pleasure of believing what we see
> Is boundless, as we wish our souls to be:

to the endearing moment when Maddalo's child "after her first shyness was worn out" can be seen "rolling billiard balls about." And I like to fantasize that just as Shelley projects his affectionate "quarrel" with Byron onto Maddalo, Crane might have dramatized his own conflicts and fashioned a Cortez out of his more severe arguments with Tate, Winters, and others. And had a good time doing it.

*

The bias in American modernism, in Pound, Williams, Moore, even Eliot, was toward a hard, sinewy, anti-poetic (non-Romantic/Victorian) style. It was an attempt to purge themselves of the afflatus of the late 19th century and make it possible for poetry to renew itself by taking on some of the materials and textures of prose.

Crane and Lowry wouldn't settle for a flattened idiom. They wanted to pull out all the stops, and didn't see why their language shouldn't be as rich and supple as that of the Elizabethans. They wouldn't accede to the implicit guidelines as to what writing at that time should be: Pound's "direct treatment of the thing"; Hemingway's "iceberg," with nine-tenths underwater.

Lowry's gesture is closer to that of Wolfe and Faulkner than his countrymen born at the same time as he— Waugh, Orwell, Auden, Spender, Day Lewis. He comments wryly on his remoteness from the world of letters in "Through the Panama."

> I am capable of conceiving of a writer today, even intrinsically a first-rate writer, who simply cannot understand, and never has been able to understand, what his fellow writers are driving at, and have been driving at, and who has always been too shy to ask. This writer feels this deficiency in himself to the point of anguish. Essentially a humble fellow, he has tried his hardest all his life to understand (though maybe still not hard enough) so that his room is full of *Partisan Reviews, Kenyon Reviews, Minotaurs, Poetry* mags, *Horizons*, even old *Dials*, of whose contents he is able to make out precisely nothing, save where an occasional contribution of his own, years and years ago,

rings a faint bell in his mind, a bell that is growing ever fainter, because to tell the truth he can no longer understand his own early work either. . . .

Despite this, he still heroically reads a few pages of William Empson's *Seven Types of Ambiguity* each night before going to sleep just to keep his hand in, as it were, and to keep up with the times.

*

Lowry wrote to Jacques Barzun that he had never read all of *Ulysses*. But he knew how it worked: that every word in the novel referred to something else, that nothing had been left to chance. So Joyce's 7 Eccles Street becomes Lowry's magical cabalistic *7* in *Under the Volcano*.

"Here we come to seven," Lowry writes to Jonathan Cape,

the fateful, the magical, the lucky good-bad number and the scene in the tower, where I write this letter. By a coincidence I moved to the tower on January 7. . . . My house burned down on June 7; when I returned to the burned site someone had branded, for some reason, the number 7 on a burned tree; why was I not a philosopher? . . . Philosophy has been dying since the days of Duns Scotus, though it continues underground, if quacking slightly. Boehme would support me when I speak of the passion for order even in the smallest things in the universe: 7 too is the number on the horse that will kill Yvonne and 7 the hour when the Consul will die . . .

And since everything in the book is doubled, trebled and quadrupled, the Consul, whose sexual shyness is telegraphed when he's caught fucking in a sand-trap on a golf course by Jacques Laruelle in the flashback in chapter one, is hurled into the ravine in chapter twelve. Every page of *Under the Volcano* expresses this tension, like the real but also symbolic rider who always seems to be losing control, drunk, "sprawling all over his mount, his stirrups lost, a feat in itself considering their size, and barely managing to hold on by the reins, though not once did he grasp the pommel to steady himself." This tension finally explodes when Yvonne is trampled to death in a dark wood by a rearing horse, as the Pleiades wheel like a transmogrified white whale. The "sharp pistol-like report, from somewhere ahead, as of a backfiring car," which she hears, is from the bullet that kills the Consul; it spooks the "riderless horse," "with number seven branded on its rump" who runs off into the forest and causes her to meet a real death in a "forest of symbols."

*

There is a dryness which draws one to Mexico. (Heraclitus says, "A dry soul is wisest and best.") All this week I built up a great thirst—how blessed a Coke seems with its heady mixture of water and sugar and caffeine. And yet, seeking relief from the blinding light in Mitla in a cavernous cantina which sells everything under the sun, I look at the bottles of Mescal, where a slice of carrot's been inserted to replace the glorious horrific worm, with a kind of longing, a thirst that's been instilled by the very maguey plant, which looks like an octopus on its back, that mescal comes from.

My disappointment in mescal did not originally stem from its smelling like ether or the hideous taste—only that the high is merely alcoholic, not hallucinatory, like mescaline.

*

Lowry's thirst found its form in what he called "a chur-
rigueresque"—florid—architecture which paralleled—
and satirized—his book's "overloaded style." He was
driven to anthropomorphize Mexico's "tall exotic plants . . .
perishing on every hand of unnecessary thirst, staggering, it almost appeared, against one another, yet
struggling like dying voluptuaries in a vision to main-
tain some final attitude of potency, or of a collective
desolate fecundity. . . ."

In Mexico, Lowry found the landscape and culture mirrored
his aesthetic concerns. His practice is congruent with
this culture where everything stands for something else—
where the full moon *is* the lopped head of a goddess.
Lowry interpreted events in his life as signs and portents and wanted them to assume symbolic significance
in his work, like the shifting shapes of the volcanoes
that reveal the mind's cliffs and falls.

> Popocatepetl loomed, pyramidal, to their right, one
> side beautifully curved as a woman's breast, the other
> precipitous, jagged, ferocious. Cloud drifts were massing
> again, high-piled, behind it. Ixtaccihautl appeared . . .

Even the serpentine ravine where the Consul is hurled
to a "dingy" death was waiting for Lowry in the "real"
Cuernavaca.

*

Spain did not transplant to Mexico. And Indian Mexico
lies like a ruin under Spanish architecture.

Ruin as final form.

All that remains of the sacred is the silence.

The value of a ruin is inseparable from how much grandeur it has lost. How pure and fabulous the projections of lost magnificence! Loss is somehow at the heart of it, loss of what was never possessed except communally.

*

I take as germane to current aesthetic practice Godard's statement that his films have a beginning, a middle, and an end, *but not necessarily in that order.*

*

Strange as it may seem now, Lowry was always in danger of being compared to writers as different as Graham Greene (*The Power and the Glory* "takes place" in Mexico and Greene's whisky priest is not so far removed from Lowry's drunken Consul) and Charles Jackson (whose *Lost Weekend* Lowry nicknamed *The Drunkard's Rigadoon*).

Archibald MacLeish made a stab at a verse epic about the conquest, but I can't see that his tepid *Conquistador* ("This is Cortés that took the famous land") is anywhere within range of the tension Crane wanted to explore.

*

Once in Mexico, Crane knew he could not escape his demons. He'd ingested, metaphorically, the worm, internalized the other, the criticism of *The Bridge* by his onetime friends and supporters (by then young old men)

Yvor Winters and Allen Tate who took Crane to task for his Whitmanian optimism, his—in Tate's words—romantic "rejection of a rational and qualitative will." Tate's "will" of intentions is a far cry from that wild conflux of energy and desire that altered the course of Western philosophy. Tate may have felt betrayed when Crane, the potential hero of the New Criticism, had blasted open the poem as self-contained object.

Crane was an optimist but not a shallow one: his optimism had nothing to do with an idealistic notion of history—it came from his ecstatic core. He sought an undivided wholeness. And drink helped him envision "new thresholds, new anatomies!" Ecstasy was the only solution he would entertain. He warred against the fallibility that might have been his own "lever of transcendence." He acted as if he owned his suffering and he refused to scrutinize it.

Paradoxically, Crane might have listened less to Whitman's vision and learned more from how Whitman expanded the self, his liberating and fictitious trope of the cosmic "I." Instead of plotting a grandiose epic, he might have paid attention to "the world dimensional," which he saw, in a Blakean sense, *through*, not merely *with*, his eyes.

Crane was never one to play his cards close to his chest. He once began a letter to Yvor Winters: "You need a good drubbing for all your talk about the whole man." He must have sensed the finality of his estrangement from Tate when he adopted a somewhat formal tone in a late letter to him: "The fact that you posit the Bridge at the end of a tradition of romanticism may prove to have been an accurate prophecy, but I don't yet feel that such a statement can be taken as a foregone conclusion. A great deal of romanticism may persist— of the sort that deserve serious consideration, I mean."

And now he recognized that his connection to God was broken, that his image of a continuous span of generations in resounding harmony was a fantasy, broken, like his sundered parentage, like the broken tower, like the tragic and abrupt breaking of Indian Mexico, when so many secrets were lost, or went underground.

The history of the conquest is a history that cannot be healed.

To write his verse epic he would have had to reconcile Mexican history and heal the quaking rift between the Spanish and the Aztec, the Catholic and the pagan, given his temperament and design. This could not be done. A broken tower is the perfect expression of this rift—as well as of themes indigenous to Crane. "The Broken Tower" is an apter image of Crane's inner life than *The Bridge* which Crane *willed* into triumphal completion.

> The bells, I say, the bells break down their tower;
> And swing I know not where. Their tongues engrave
> Membrane through marrow, my long-scattered score
> Of broken intervals . . . And I, their sexton slave!

In a sense, Crane's Mexican project was doomed because he planned it in advance. And so it was with immense sadness that I read of Crane's desire to write the history of the conquest in verse because the project put him at a remove from his own life, while his letters from

Mexico are steeped in the spirit of the place. They show how intensely Crane, always the symbolist in his poems, was present in everyday life—and a creature of enthusiasms.

> I rushed from the bar where I was drinking tequila—
> up the dark corridors and stairways of the church
> and on to the roof, expecting to be thrown over when
> I got there, but still too excited to resist. . . . Can
> you imagine the strange, strange mixture, the musi-
> cians standing with their faces toward the high dark
> cliff surmounted by the temple of the old barbaric
> god that they were propitiating, and stopping every
> 15 minutes while the sextons rang out the call of the
> Cross over the same dark valley!

*

When the fit was not upon him Crane had a strangely amicable relationship to his environment. And the effect of his poetry is inseparable from its unforced exuberance, sweetness and charm, as when, in "Repose of Rivers," "the singular nestings in the hills/Where beavers learn stitch and tooth."

"Be reconciled with your world," Williams urged his fellow poets: and, in many ways, Crane was—but he never found a way to consistently bridge his perceptions, to join the grand and the commonplace, aspiration and actuality, in a sort of mystical fusion. Crane's problem was how to recover from that moment of ecstasy, that moment of pure duration—how to get through the rest of the day or night without seeking to recapture that state whose precise nature it is not to be in time.

Crane is the man who rose before dawn to meet the

bell ringer; who rode the wild bell ropes before writing:

> The bell-rope that gathers God at dawn
> Dispatches me as though I dropped down the knell
> Of a spent day—to wander the cathedral lawn
> From pit to crucifix, feet chill on steps from hell.

His metaphysical lines had a root in physical life, in
the life of the body, which, Donne reminds us, "makes
the minde." That is why when Crane failed to make
the imaginative leap he needed, a leap which would
have demanded Houdini-like mental resources, his next
leap was from the prow of the *Orizaba* into the sea,
which welcomed him, where he could be whole again.
He'd already noted in "Voyages" that "The bottom of
the sea is cruel." He'd already written his underwater
epitaph in "At Melville's Tomb":

> The dice of drowned men's bones bequeath
> An embassy.

*

Crane set his acoustical register at the highest pitch,
as in the layered sonics in the opening passage of "The
Harbor Dawn":

> Insistently through sleep—a tide of voices—
> They meet you listening midway in your dream,
> The long, tired sounds, fog-insulated noises:
> Gongs in white surplices, beshrouded wails,
> Far strum of fog horns . . . signals dispersed in veils.
>
> And when a truck will lumber past the wharves
> As winch engines begin throbbing on some deck;

Or a drunken stevedor's howl and thud below
Comes echoing alley-upward through dim snow.

But where could Crane go from this exhausted gor-
geousness, this plenitude of impressions? Crane ideal-
ized poetry. He resisted taking the next step into further impurity. He denied himself access to the errors
that might have comprised the work. The highest note
is not the only note (any more than we would like to
listen to an opera in which only a coloratura soprano
sings), and Crane had the heart and mind to expand,
to harden and see the world through a crueler eye,
without sacrificing the rising swell of the ecstasy he
strove to recapture as in "Voyages":

> —And yet this great wink of eternity,
> Of rimless floods, unfettered leewardings,
> Samite sheeted and processioned where
> Her undinal vast belly moonward bends,
> Laughing the wrapt inflections of our love;
>
> *
>
> Bind us in time, O Seasons clear, and awe.
> O minstrel galleons of Carib fire,
> Bequeath us to no earthly shore until
> Is answered in the vortex of our grave
> The seal's wide spindrift gaze toward paradise.

*

Lowry was a novelist in search of a new form and he
saw man—as in his letters he frequently quoted Ortega
y Gasset saying—as like a novelist, making up his life
as he goes along, trying to find his vocation.

Lowry, in adopting the Flaubertian ideal of language, applied it to the writing of essentially romantic works. But Lowry had a special problem. He was a novelist who, as he admitted, could not create characters apart from himself, one who had no access to the idea of other people. His was an inward gaze.

His fatal defect as a novelist was that he was only interested, *finally*, in himself. Everyone in *Under the Volcano* is another facet of the Consul's personality. By creating a character with whom he didn't share any external occupational hazards, Lowry adapted the formal principles of the "objective" novel, and then put himself, in the guise of the romantic figure of the Consul (or later, Sigbjørn Wilderness), at the center of the novel.

(It is as though Flaubert had tried to write a *bildungsroman* in which the author would "identify" with a "positive hero": the artist in him would have been at war with the lyricism of his work-in-progress.)

*

But writing *Under the Volcano* closed the door to Lowry for future work that had the possibility within itself to be completed within a finite stretch of time. In the ten years in which he lived after the publication of *Under the Volcano* he wrote voluminously and finished (much less published) almost nothing. This sense of failure was not appeased by having created a masterpiece because the essential project wasn't working. (Lowry's "blocks" took the form of loggorhea.) "Do I contradict myself?" I hope so. Because this is dangerous ground. It verges on arrogance to say that in writing *Under the*

Volcano in the way he did, as evidenced in his letters, Lowry cut himself off from his future.

*

Lowry might have taken the success of his marvelous novella, "Through the Panama," with its judicious merger of journal and journey—its carefully delineated voyage—as a sign that he was onto something; he might have found a form that would have allowed him to write the books he had to write, which would be without some of the strain and forced quality of his unfinished epic attempts. He was even partially sympathetic with an argument in which *Portrait of the Artist as a Young Man* was flawed because there was not enough differentiation between Joyce and Daedalus.

In certain passages of Crane's poetry and many of his letters, and in Lowry's prose, especially "Through the Panama," you sense an opening, a manner of expression that seems native, if not natural, to the writer. Yet the writing I'm referring to has little to do really with the aesthetic and the drive behind the modernist masterpieces with which Crane and Lowry were competing—the works that set the standard for contemporary practice. Both men wrote elaborate descriptions and defenses of their work ("At Melville's Tomb," *The Bridge, Under the Volcano*), that stand among the great literary letters of all time. In fact, the descriptions in these letters are almost too schematic to be entirely believable: they almost go so far as if to say *no one can tell me anything about my work which I haven't put in there.* I am aware of the contexts in which they wrote these letters: they were trying to convince patrons and publishers of the unassailable rightness of their works. These letters indicate that the process of writing these works left little to chance. And if you abolish chance you abolish possibility, and the next work, still percolating in the unconscious, becomes an endangered species.

*

"I shall . . . give my brush rein," says Kenko, a 14th century Japanese poet and essayist who worked in a form called the Zuihitsu, (which means—"follow your brush"—). I like to imagine Crane and Lowry taking nourishment and courage from his example, as say, Philip Guston could from Fra Angelico. "Leaving something incomplete makes it interesting, and gives one the feeling that there is room for growth."

*

The writer must create the form anew in order to work in it.

*

"One reaches certain truths," Natalie Sarraute says,

"but truths that are already known. At a level that's already known. One can describe the Soviet reality in Tolstoy's manner, but one will never manage to penetrate it further than Tolstoy did with the aristocratic society that he described. It will remain at the same level of the psyche as Anna Karenina or Prince Bolkonsky if you use the form that Tolsoy used. If you employ the form of Dostoyevsky, you will arrive at another level, which will always be Dostoyevsky's level, whatever the society you describe. That's my idea. If you want to penetrate further, you must abandon

both of them and go look for something else. Form
and content are the same thing. If you take a certain
form, you attain a certain content with that form,
not any other. . . . Each time has to find its form. *It's
the sensation that impels the form"* (my emphasis).

*

Because of its relative wholeness, Teotihuacan is the
least ruined and least interesting of the ruins I have
seen in Mexico. I had no burning desire to go back to
it after twenty years but my wife wanted to go and I
had nothing better to do, and a restless curiosity impelled me. Besides, it would be nice to see it unescorted
by a guide and without time constrictions. Years before, I had made the mistake of taking a guide, an
impatient man dressed in a black suit as if for a funeral, who insisted that we visit the gift shop at the
godawful shrine of the Virgin of Guadalupe, wasting
valuable time we could have spent at the pyramids. I
saw women crawling on bloody knees toward the shrine—
at least they wore scarves in their hair to keep off the
sun. And the sun in Mexico is direct and ubiquitous.
Everything, even the canary yellow walls of cemeter-
ies, reflects the ferocity of the sun.

*

Mexico encourages ecstatic negation. I had the sense,
once, at Chichén Itzá, that when you reached the top
steps of the pyramid you were meant to hurtle into
space, into the nowhere—that endless space was the
next date on the Aztec calendar. In the Mexican "universe of time" (Paz) there is no duration. The only time
is eternal time.

*

I don't need my son's erect painted reptile, the up-sweep of his tail, to remember Mexico, or where we bought it—on a high hill in Oaxaca as the sun still swept across the valley in broad, swift strokes; and the police eyed us as we fondled serapes and beheld well-wrought pottery, and that pinkish glow—Oaxacan— was on the stones: everything was imprisoned in light. I stood looking down the steep street toward the zocalo and up into the hills—past the market's vats of fly-infested pulque, past the barrels of fried pork rind, past the wicker baskets brimful with dark, gnarled, roots and branches, past tatters of the word "Olmec" on crumbling walls, past ragged gates, and scorched, disfigured streets drenched in the smell of garlic and cayenne, past the ordered and chaotic light in the late Rufino Tamayo's small, pristine museum where tor-rents pour down throught the open roof and soak the courtyard. The light curved space—yet there was something sinister and menacing about it too, this lost light, lashing the streets, articulating shadows and creases, as an-other day was coming to an end in Oaxaca.

I tried to imagine what the body of Lowry's work might have been and it is at that moment I am most aware of the lack of a social matrix. His character(s) are al-ways adrift and far from their native land. Lowry, a novelist of the self and of consciousness, would have needed to thicken the broth of *The Voyage that Never Ends* by attempting to explore his own childhood. His friends talk about how his face clouded over when-ever the subject of his family arose. Childhood may have been too painful for him to reenter, but could it have been any worse than what he afterward endured, and the repercussions of his romance with the bottle?

*

It is difficult to sustain an orotund note, an elevated, hieratic tone, "in the bleak time," when, as Ammons puts it in his nonchalant way in "Doubling the Nerve," you can:

> look for no cooperation
> from the birds: crows show up, black blatant
> clarions in the gawky branches, to dominate
> the rain's dark

They both felt artistically bankrupt, bereft when they died. Crane wrote one of his greatest shorter poems in Mexico but it wasn't what he set out to do. The Consul, like Casaubon, is unable to complete his secret work: his definitive tome becomes his tomb. When Lowry quotes—intentionally misquotes—Marlowe's *Faustus* when Jacques Laruelle, remembering the Consul as he looks into a book of Elizabethan plays, reads: "Then will I headlong

> fly into the earth.
> Earth, gape! it will not harbor me.

Only Faustus had not quite said that. He looked more closely at the passage. Faustus had said. 'Then will I headlong run into the earth,' and 'O, no, it will not—'. That was not so bad. Under the circumstances it was not so bad as to fly." Lowry hacks a few consoling syllables—signifying delay—out of Marlowe's mighty line, and makes the pain more acute than—

> Then will I headlong run into the earth.
> Gape earth! *O no*, it will not harbor me.

*

Mexico supplied Crane and Lowry with the symbols they needed, but it did not leave them with a way out. Lowry, in moving from Cuernavaca to Dollartan, Canada, imagined he could substitute a heaven for a hell, cutting himself off, with strange psychic deliberation, from the purgatory of his past. Where Beckett chose the inevitability of "failure" as the condition of the artist in mid-century and used it (plying contradiction!) as a goad and challenge to "go on" both Crane and Lowry were condemned to chronicle a Dantean—upward movement of the soul—"toward paradise."

*

I knew that Crane and Lowry were troubled men, but when I was first reading them, when still in my teens, I had no sense that their crises might have had anything to do with their lives as artists—I couldn't see through the rosy tints of my esteem for what they *had* done.

The same is true of my idealization of a couple whom I saw play a variety of classic roles in repertory at the same time I had first discovered *Under the Volcano* and *The Bridge.*

Back in Manhattan, looking up from my table at a sidewalk café on Broadway, I notice the actor walk by. When I first saw him in the lead role of *'Tis Pity She's a Whore,* he was almost too pretty for the part of Giovanni, his then sandy hair parted Prince Valiant style down the middle, but he was very good, and I remember now the scene where he cuts out his sister Annabella's heart and holds it out to the audience—a bloody gory pulpy heart—very *real.*

> Gio.   The glory of my deed
> Darkened the mid-day sun, made noon as night.
> You came to feast, my lords, with dainty fair:
> I came to feast too; but I digged for food
> In a much richer mine than gold or stone
> Of any value balanced; *'tis a heart,*
> *A heart, my lords, in which mine is entombed:*

The actor has since perfected degenerate roles, white trash killers, sinister businessmen, etc. And at this moment I think of him holding out the heart with an Aztec innocence—it is already set within the context of a *feast.*

> Ann.   Be not deceived, my brother;
> This banquet is an harbinger of death
> To you and me; resolve yourself it is,
> And be prepared to welcome it.

In other words, in his pre-conquest, "Aztec," phase he played Ford and Shakespeare and Chekhov and Pirandello and when he "grew up," that is, metaphorically speaking, after the conquest, he played villains in mediocre movies and made a lot of money.

It is as if the actor's lines predicted his life. Once he cut out his sister's heart, *his* heart, "entombed" in it, no longer retained its purity of ambition. His act, *in the play,* put him in the role of Mexico after the conquest. Before that Giovanni heartily and willfully violates the incest taboo.

In the mid-nineteen seventies, when I lived in Greenwich Village, I used to see the actor's wife, herself a well-known stage actress, pushing a baby carriage on West 4th Street or in Abington Square Park on Hudson

Street from where you could glimpse the river, or having tea, with her baby in tow, at Arnold's Turtle.

She seemed absolutely at home on stage. Her gentle and quiet and understated demeanor placed her at the center of the audience's attention, like the eye of a hurricane.

The play I saw the couple in that year had such a deep effect on my life I had to speak to her. One day I overtook her and the stroller and told her the theater never had such magic for me before or since as when I saw her and her husband in 'Tis Pity She's a Whore.

"But I hated it," she said. "It was a terrible year, the worst year of my life, I'd never do repertory again. The conditions were terrible, the pay was terrible, we'd no sooner mastered one thing and we were off onto another."

*

The conversation caused a rupture in reality for me. I had misjudged everything, I had projected my then 18/19-year-old consciousness and innocence and experience onto her 28/29-year-old consciousness. It had never occurred to me that the circumstance could matter, that the pay (give or take a few hundred a month) could matter when you were performing Shakespeare and Ford and Chekhov and Pirandello to rapt audiences. I could never have predicted that the actor would switch physically from being an Adonis to a Magwitch in so short a time, from a perhaps too ethereal presence to an ugly, brutal, distorted one, the quintessential evil scum like those portrayed by Strother Martin in Westerns like The Wild Bunch.

The actress stuck to her guns, performing mainly great classical roles and remained known to few outside that sphere. She did not utter her words in anger. She was a gentle, serene presence, even as she quietly excoriated her repertory year. I realize now that she was probably in a fury at having been abandoned by her husband. So it was in essence *her* heart the actor gouged out of her chest in a play written only some 70 years after Cortez arrived in Tenochtitlan.

The actor, Artaud says, is an athlete of the heart.

The actor crosses over the boundary between the living and the dead.

> CRUELTY. Without an element of cruelty at the foundation of every spectacle, the theater is not possible. In the state of degeneracy, in which we live, it is through the skin that metaphysics will be made to reenter our minds.

*

From Ford's *The Broken Heart*:

> Armostes: Quiet
> These vain unruly passions, which will render ye
> Into a madness.
>
> Orgilus: Griefs will have their vent.

*

The cutting out of human hearts was also a Provencal practice. Pound deftly adapted the story of Guilhem De Cabestan in *Canto IV*.

> "It is Cabestan's heart in the dish."
> "It is Cabestan's heart in the dish."
> "No other taste shall change this."

Then the Spanish came and put a stop to Aztec sacrifices. Yet it is this direct savage reality of the Aztecs and Jacobeans that drew Crane and Lowry to Mexico. But they had it in their mind to become something better.

Both Crane and Lowry tried for Elizabethan grandeur within a decadent Jacobean frame. That is one reason for the strain you feel in their work, a strain that seems to say—*if the world were different the work would be different*. The "fallen world" would not accept the burden of their praise—beyond a certain point.

> Wer immer strebend sich bemuht, den können wir
>   erlösen.
> Whoever unceasingly strives upward . . . him we can
>   save.
>
> (Goethe, *Faust*)

The irony of Lowry's epigraph is that he and Crane, in the verticality of their striving, lost sight of the advantages of being where they were in reality—"in the last bloody ditch where," as Beckett once put it, "there is no choice but to sing."

Mark Rudman was born in New York City, and grew up in the Midwest and West. He has received the Academy of American Poets Prize, the *Denver Quarterly* Award, the Max Hayward Award for his translation of Boris Pasternak's *My Sister—Life*, fellowships in poetry from the Ingram Merrill Foundation and the New York Foundation of the Arts, and in translation of poetry from the P.E.N. Translation Center. His most recent book of poems, *The Nowhere Steps*, appeared in 1990. *By Contraries: Poems 1970–84* appeared in 1987. His other books include a critical study, *Robert Lowell: An Introduction to the Poetry*, and a translation of Bohdan Boychuk's selected poems, *Memories of Love*, done in collaboration with the author. He is currently translating Euripides' *Trojan Women* for the Oxford Series of Greek Tragedies. His book-length poem, *Rider*, is forthcoming.

Mark Rudman's poems have appeared in a wide number of magazines and anthologies including *The Atlantic Monthly, Harper's, The New Yorker, The New Directions Annual, The Paris Review*, and *Best American Poetry 1989*. His essays have appeared in the anthologies *Best American Essays 1991* and *Conversant Essays*, and *American Poetry Review, Boulevard, The New York Times Book Review*, and *Threepenny Review*. He lives in New York City where he is Adjunct Professor in the writing programs at Columbia University and New York University and is editor of the literary magazine *Pequod*.

THE TYPE IS PALATINO, ORIGINALLY DESIGNED BY HERMANN ZAPF
AND REPRODUCED ELECTRONICALLY FOR COMPUTER

❦

BOOK DESIGN BY LYSA MCDOWELL
COVER IMAGE BY SUSAN LAUFER
PRINTING BY EDWARDS BROTHERS